CHRISTIANITY AND ROMAN SOCIETY

Early Christianity in the context of Roman society raises important questions for historians, sociologists of religion and theologians alike. This work explores the differing perspectives arising from a changing social and academic culture. Key issues on early Christianity are addressed, such as how early Christian accounts of pagans, Jews and heretics can be challenged and the degree to which Christian groups offered support to their members and to those in need. The work examines how non-Christians reacted to the spectacle of martyrdom and to Christian reverence for relics. Questions are also raised on why some Christians encouraged others to abandon wealth, status and gender-roles for extreme ascetic lifestyles and on whether Christian preachers trained in classical culture offered moral education to all or only to the social elite. The interdisciplinary and thematic approach offers the student of early Christianity a comprehensive treatment of its role and influence in Roman society.

GILLIAN CLARK is Professor of Ancient History at the University of Bristol. She has written extensively on Christianity and classical culture and her previous publications include *Augustine: Confessions Books I–IV* (editor) (Cambridge University Press, 1995).

KEY THEMES IN ANCIENT HISTORY

EDITORS

P. A. Cartledge
Clare College, Cambridge

P. D. A. Garnsey
Jesus College, Cambridge

Key Themes in Ancient History aims to provide readable, informed and original studies of various basic topics, designed in the first instance for students and teachers of Classics and Ancient History, but also for those engaged in related disciplines. Each volume is devoted to a general theme in Greek, Roman, or, where appropriate, Graeco-Roman history, or to some salient aspect or aspects of it. Besides indicating the state of current research in the relevant area, authors seek to show how the theme is significant for our own as well as ancient culture and society. By providing books for courses that are oriented around themes it is hoped to encourage and stimulate promising new developments in teaching and research in ancient history.

Other books in the series

Death-ritual and social structure in classical antiquity, by Ian Morris
0 521 37465 0 (hardback), 0 521 37611 4 (paperback)

Literacy and orality in ancient Greece, by Rosalind Thomas
0 521 37346 8 (hardback), 0 521 37742 0 (paperback)

Slavery and society at Rome, by Keith Bradley
0 521 37287 9 (hardback), 0 521 37887 7 (paperback)

Law, violence, and community in classical Athens, by David Cohen
0 521 38167 3 (hardback), 0 521 38837 6 (paperback)

Public order in ancient Rome, by Wilfried Nippel
0 521 38327 7 (hardback), 0 521 38749 3 (paperback)

Friendship in the classical world, by David Konstan
0 521 45402 6 (hardback), 0 521 45998 2 (paperback)

Sport and society in ancient Greece, by Mark Golden
0 521 49698 5 (hardback), 0 521 49790 6 (paperback)

Food and society in classical antiquity, by Peter Garnsey
0 521 64182 9 (hardback), 0 521 64588 3 (paperback)

Banking and business in the Roman world, by Jean Andreau
0 521 38031 6 (hardback), 0 521 38932 1 (paperback)

Roman law in context, by David Johnston
0 521 63046 0 (hardback), 0 521 63961 1 (paperback)

Religions of the ancient Greeks, by Simon Price
0 521 38201 7 (hardback), 0 521 38867 8 (paperback)

Ancient Greece: using evidence, by Pamela Bradley
0 521 79646 6 (paperback)

Ancient Rome: using evidence, by Pamela Bradley
0 521 79391 2 (paperback)

CHRISTIANITY AND ROMAN SOCIETY

GILLIAN CLARK

CAMBRIDGE
UNIVERSITY PRESS

PUBLISHED BY THE PRESS SYNDICATE OF THE UNIVERSITY OF CAMBRIDGE
The Pitt Building, Trumpington Street, Cambridge, United Kingdom

CAMBRIDGE UNIVERSITY PRESS
The Edinburgh Building, Cambridge, CB2 2RU, UK
32 Avenue of the Americas, New York, NY 10013–2473, USA
477 Williamstown Road, Port Melbourne, VIC 3207, Australia
Ruiz de Alarcón 13, 28014 Madrid, Spain
Dock House, The Waterfront, Cape Town 8001, South Africa

http://www.cambridge.org
Information on this title: www.cambridge.org/9780521633864

First published 2004
Reprinted 2006 (twice)

Printed in the United Kingdom at the University Press, Cambridge

Typeface Adobe Garamond 11/12.5 pt.   *System* LATEX 2$_\varepsilon$ [TB]

A catalogue record for this book is available from the British Library

ISBN-13 978-0-521-63386-4 paperback
ISBN-10 0-521-63386-9 paperback

ISBN-13 978-0-521-63310-9 hardback
ISBN-10 0-521-63310-9 hardback

JCJM

emerito non otioso

Ars mea, multorum es quos saecula prisca tulerunt:
sed nova te brevitas asserit esse meam.
Omnia cum veterum sint explorata libellis,
multa loqui breviter sit novitatis opus.
Te relegat iuvenis, quem garrula pagina terret,
aut siquem paucis seria nosse iuvat;
te longinqua petens comitem sibi ferre viator
ne dubitet, parvo pondere multa vehens.
        (Cassiodorus, *De orthographia* 146, quoting Phocas)

This book's the work of many, but it's short,
And that is new and shows it to be mine.
What's new is putting briefly all that work.
Long books scare students: this is one for them,
And anyone who likes some serious thoughts
Concisely said. Long-distance travellers
Will find its content well above its weight.

Contents

Preface

This book draws on research, editorial work, and teaching at the universities of Liverpool and Bristol. It owes much to my first experience of Bristol teaching, shared with Neville Morley, in the academic year 2000/1. Our final-year seminar on 'Christianity and Roman society' included students for whom Christianity is an interesting aspect of the Roman empire and students for whom Christianity is a living faith. I am grateful to them all, for their intellectual curiosity, for the consideration they showed each other, and for making it clear that I had accepted too easily many things that need to be explained. The final draft benefited from another final-year seminar, in autumn 2003, shared this time with Richard Goodrich. The book attempts to outline some of the possible explanations for things that need to be explained, and to direct its readers to others. It is, of course, a snapshot of fast-moving scholarship, from one person's perspective, in a specific context of place and time. It is a book that could go on being written for years to come, as new information and new interpretations are published; but no doubt the series editors feel that it has gone on being written for quite long enough.

There is an immense range of published work, from different national and religious traditions, on the evidence for Roman, Jewish and Christian history and religion in the early centuries CE. I am a classical historian with a special interest in late antiquity, not a theologian or a New Testament specialist or a Judaist. As a member of the Church of England, I recognise how much diversity there is in even one Christian tradition. As a classicist I know Greek and Latin, but not Hebrew and Aramaic, Syriac and Coptic and Ethiopic, Georgian and Armenian and Old Slavonic, all of which are important for the history of Christianity in the world that was dominated by the Roman empire. I find the late fourth and early fifth centuries particularly interesting, because of the classically trained Christian bishops who tried to make their scriptures and their faith intelligible to anyone who would come to church and listen, and who used their skills of rhetoric and networking to help the poor. I do not have the expertise to take the story much further, but others are working on later Christian writings, on late antique Jewish texts, on the kingdoms that succeeded Rome in the early medieval West, and on the later history of Byzantium and its interactions with Islam. I have kept to Greek and Latin in the Roman empire and the first five centuries of Christianity, with much gratitude to those whose knowledge and understanding has helped to supply some of the gaps in my own. Debts to individuals are not forgotten, but really are too numerous to mention. I have consistently learned from co-editing, with Andrew Louth, the monograph series Oxford Early Christian Studies; from co-editing, with Mary Whitby and Mark Humphries, the late-antique series Translated Texts for Historians; from sharing in the Shifting Frontiers in Late Antiquity network started by Ralph Mathisen; and from reading the work of the doctoral students whose commitment in difficult times takes this subject forward. Peter Garnsey and Paul Cartledge, editors of Key Themes, showed impressive patience as bureaucratic demands disrupted the teaching and research of all British academics; they also made valuable comments on the final draft. I am responsible for the translations and for the remaining errors.

In writing this book, I have often remembered a student I taught twenty years ago, who had entered her religious order in Ireland before the reforms of the Second Vatican Council (1965). Appealed to on questions of doctrine or practice, she could usually find an answer; but sometimes she would gently shake her head and say 'It makes you wonder what can we have been thinking of.' We do, sometimes, make progress.

Bristol, Epiphany 2004

CHAPTER I

Introduction

Do not conform to the world around you, but be transformed by your new way of thinking, so that you find out what is God's will.

(Paul of Tarsus, Romans 12.2, mid-first century)

Christians do not differ from other people in where they live, or how they talk, or in their lifestyle. They do not live in private cities, or speak a special language, or follow a peculiar way of life. Their doctrine is not an invention of inquisitive and restless thinkers; they do not champion human assertions as some people do. They live where they happen to live, in Greek or foreign cities, they follow local custom in clothing and food and daily life, yet their citizenship is of a remarkable kind. They live in their own homelands, but as resident foreigners. They share everything as citizens, and put up with everything as foreigners.

(*Letter to Diognetus*, author unknown, second century)

So this heavenly city, while living in exile on earth, summons citizens from every nation and collects a society of foreigners who speak every language; it is not concerned for what is different in the customs, laws and institutions by which earthly peace is sought or maintained. The city does not rescind or destroy any of these, but preserves and observes everything, different though it may be in different nations, that tends to one and the same end, that is, earthly peace, and that does not obstruct the religion which teaches worship of one true and highest God.

(Augustine, *City of God* 19.17)

How did a tiny, politically suspect, religious splinter group become the dominant religion of the Roman world? This is one of the great historical questions, for Christianity was part of the Roman legacy to medieval Europe, and Europeans took Christianity far beyond the limits of the Roman empire. At the start of the third millennium, Christianity is still a major world-wide religion. But in the secular British university system, the majority of students have no religious commitment, and are aware that their education in a pluralist 'post-Christian' society has told them very little about what it might mean to call oneself Christian. The questions that students ask have shaped this book. As the quotations at the head of this chapter show, the first Christians were Romans, in the sense that they lived in the Roman empire and had a more or less close relationship, depending on their local culture and language, with the dominant Roman culture. From 212 all free inhabitants of the empire were formally Roman citizens, subject in principle, but with variations in practice, to Roman law and taxation and religious obligations. So when Christianity began, just how different was it from the other religious options of the Roman world, that is, the world ruled by Rome and formed by the cultures of Greece and Rome? Did Christianity change the world, or did Roman institutions and ways of thinking shape Christianity?

But what is meant by 'Christianity'? The simple answer is that Christians live by the teachings of Jesus Christ, but they have interpreted those teachings in many ways. How can other people identify a Christian? Does 'being Christian' depend on behaviour, such as forgiveness and active charity; or on religious practice, such as churchgoing; or on personal religious experience, such as prayer; or on acknowledging the authority of specific texts, or belief-statements, or church leaders, in understanding the relationship of human beings to God? Was Christianity always, as it so painfully is in some parts of today's world, a matter of identifying with one group and rejecting or fighting others? Is Christianity at the start of the third millennium still shaped by ethics and theology, social assumptions and traditions, cultural and political divisions inherited from the Roman world in which it began? This introductory chapter briefly surveys the relationship of Christianity to Roman society, and changing perspectives on that relationship in later historical writing. The chapters that follow develop some of the most important themes.

Chapter 2, 'Christians and others', investigates the problem of sources and the distinctions that historians have inherited from early Christian writings: Christians and pagans, Christians and Jews, Christians and heretics. Most of the sources for early Christianity have survived because they were acceptable to the Christians whose theology prevailed. How then can we reconstruct the perspective of people who thought they were Christians but whose theology was classed as heresy, or of people who were not Christians, or of the silent majority who did not write about their beliefs? Were the distinctions so clear in practice? Were Christians and non-Christians divided only by misunderstanding and polemic, or were there fundamental differences of beliefs and values? Did Christian groups offer an alternative family, a level of emotional and practical support, or of moral and religious teaching, that was not available in other religious options? Why would anyone choose the one religious option that carried the risk of an appalling public death?

Chapter 3, 'The blood of the martyrs', asks why, and to what extent, Romans persecuted Christians, and how the penalties inflicted by Roman law shaped the identity of the church. How did non-Christian Romans react to the deaths of martyrs, and how did Christians reinterpret those deaths? How did fragments of dead bodies become holy and powerful relics? What happened to the ideal of martyrdom after persecution ended in the early fourth century?

Chapter 4, 'Body and soul', considers the impact of martyrdom, and of philosophical tradition, on early Christian teaching about the body. Why did (some) Christians reject the ties of family and society, and why did they argue that the best kind of Christian was a celibate living in austerity or even deprivation? Why did Christians develop single-sex communities for men and, uniquely in Roman society, for women? How far did Christian asceticism differ from philosophical asceticism, in ways of living and in ways of thinking about oneself?

Chapter 5, 'People of the Book', considers the impact of a shared sacred text, namely Jewish scripture with the addition of selected (and disputed) Christian texts. What difference did it make that Christians had such a text? Could anyone come to church and hear regular religious and moral teaching, sometimes from highly educated preachers? Was this a unique opportunity in Roman culture, or was it one aspect of a general concern for texts? Could Christianity have been incorporated into the range of religious wisdom on offer in the Roman world?

Chapter 6, 'Triumph, disaster or adaptation?', focuses on the fourth and early fifth centuries. At the start of the fourth century Christianity was a persecuted religion; by the start of the fifth century it was the only approved religion. How did the extraordinary become the ordinary? Was there already little to choose between Christianity and Roman society, or did Christianity adapt its teachings to a new social role? Did Christians persecute in their turn, oppressing Jews, heretics and pagans, or had pagans already lost commitment to traditional religion? Did Christian charity make the invisible poor visible, or did Christian bishops appropriate the role and the prestige of local patrons? Is this the end of Roman society, of authentic Christianity, of both or of neither?

BEGINNINGS

Jesus of Nazareth, known to his followers as Jesus Christ, was born in the reign of Augustus, the first Roman emperor, in an obscure district of the Roman-ruled territory then called Judaea. The precise date of his birth is uncertain, but it was not far off the year now called AD 1, the starting-point of the Christian calendar.[1] *Iudaea* is Latin for 'Jewish' (land or province): Jesus and many of his first followers were Jews, a fact often disregarded until the mid-twentieth century. These first followers are called disciples, from Latin *discipulus*, 'student'; this is one example among many of Christian vocabulary derived from the Greek and Latin of early Christian texts. Jesus also taught people who were not Jews, for the population of Judaea was ethnically and religiously diverse. Judaea was not an important base for Roman legions, and its Roman governor was not of the highest rank. It had some garrisons of auxiliary troops, mostly local recruits, and paid taxes to the Roman government. Some of its inhabitants accepted this as they had accepted other foreign rulers, some found it politically and religiously unacceptable.[2]

At about the age of thirty, in or near the year 33, Jesus was crucified outside Jerusalem, on the orders of Pontius Pilatus, the governor appointed by Augustus' successor Tiberius. He was tied to a wooden cross, secured by nails driven through wrists and ankles, and left to die – of thirst, exposure or heart failure, depending on the conditions and his physical strength. Roman law authorised this cruel form of execution, but it was usually reserved for slaves and rebels. Jesus may have been accused of rebellion. According to his followers, he was crucified between two *leistai* (Mark 15.27). This word is traditionally translated 'thieves', but it often implied the kind of outlaws who are called freedom fighters by their friends and bandits, or terrorists, by their enemies (Schwartz 2001: 89–81). The followers of Jesus said that the Sanhedrin, the Jewish council, condemned him for blasphemy, and also accused him of subversion (Luke 22.66–23.5). The notice on his cross (John 19.20) identified him as Jesus of Nazareth, king of the Jews, and was written in Latin, Greek and Hebrew,[3] the three official languages of the region. His followers believed that he was the Messiah, God's anointed: in

---

[1] Dionysius Exiguus, a monk from Scythia (South Russia), calculated this date in the sixth century. AD stands for *anno domini*, Latin for 'in the year of the Lord'; CE, 'Common Era' (see below), is a widely used alternative.

[2] Fredriksen 2000 for Judaea in the time of Jesus; Schwartz 2001 for Jewish society over a longer period; Rajak 2001 for Jewish relationships with Greek and Roman culture.

[3] This probably means the local language, Aramaic, not the classical Hebrew of the Jewish scriptures.

Greek, *christos*. In Jewish tradition, anointing with oil symbolised kingship, and prophecies foretold the Messiah, but there were many interpretations of when he would come and what he would do. From the earliest Christian writings (perhaps as early as the mid-first century) to the present day, Christians have tried to find ways of expressing who Jesus was, what was his relationship to God whom he called 'Father', and what it means for the relationship of all human beings to God.[4]

Roman law executed Jesus, and Christians had to contend with the argument that they worshipped a crucified man, a human being who had been condemned to one of the cruellest and most degrading penalties of Roman law. But the Roman authorities did not hunt down his followers, and Christian missionaries spread their teachings throughout the Mediterranean world with the help of Roman roads, Roman imperial control, and Roman acceptance of religious diversity. The Roman empire, in the early centuries CE, made no attempt to establish a universal cult or sacred text or priesthood or belief-statement: nor did it repress cults, unless they offended against Roman religious feeling (most obviously by human sacrifice, ch. 2) or against public order. Emperors, living and dead, were variously honoured in association with gods, but there was no empire-wide 'imperial cult' with a system of priesthood and ritual (Beard–North–Price 1998: 1.348–63). Instead of integrated universal cults, there were 'family resemblances' of cult practice: animal sacrifice at altars, land or buildings sacred to the god, cult-images and offerings. It was relatively easy to identify a local deity, such as Sul in Britain or Bel in Palmyra, with one of the widely recognised Roman gods.

Cities had local traditions about the cults that the gods required them to maintain; modern writers call these 'civic' cults. Local benefactors funded the rituals and sacred places of these cults, and were often rewarded with the honour of priesthood. The duties of a priest might be no more than an annual sacrifice, perhaps with a brief preliminary abstinence from sex or from certain foods. Very few priesthoods required a change in lifestyle. People who did not hold priesthoods had no formal religious obligations, though their neighbours might think them anti-social if they did not take part in the festivals that honoured their local deities. If they wished, they could also follow one or more of the 'elective' cults ('elective' is another useful modern term) that were maintained by groups of worshippers. In most cases, it would be difficult to tell that someone belonged to such a

---

[4] Fredriksen 2000 discusses early Christian interpretations in their historical and religious context; Ward 2000 surveys interpretations of core Christian beliefs.

cult, unless he or she was seen at a place of worship of an unfamiliar god, taking part in a ceremony, revering an image, or, sometimes, observing specific rules of lifestyle.

Judaism was a special case, both because of its monotheism and because it is an ethnic as well as a religious category. Jewish monotheism, that is, belief that there is one and only one god, was not compatible with traditional religion or with 'divine honours' for emperors, and the customs derived from Jewish scripture marked Jews as different from others. Some Romans thought that male circumcision was genital mutilation, and many were puzzled by refusal to eat pork, the cheapest available meat. There were bizarre stories about the jealous Jewish god who insisted on these customs, required sacrifice only at his temple in Jerusalem, and would not allow his worshippers to acknowledge other gods (Rives 1995). Judaism was also exceptional in providing a religious motive for rebellion, against the control of Jewish territory by idolatrous Romans. Jews who lived elsewhere, but sent money for the upkeep of the Jerusalem Temple, were sometimes suspected not just of divided loyalties, but of financing rebellion. But there were also positive responses to Judaism. Romans who were interested in philosophy respected Jews for their monotheism, their refusal to make images of their god, and their adherence to their ancient law. Jews offered sacrifice, even if it was only to one god and at one temple, for as long as the Temple stood, and they were willing to offer sacrifice for the well-being of the emperor. Even when Jews faced social discrimination, or outright hostility, they could claim that Roman law permitted their meetings for worship, and that their forms of worship, including their study of ancient sacred texts, were recognisable as religion or as philosophy (ch. 2, ch. 5).

Christianity benefited from Roman tolerance of Judaism, for early Christian groups, according to Christian texts, often began in Jewish synagogues (Greek *sunagōgē*, 'meeting-place') or among the gentile sympathisers that Jews called 'godfearers' (J. Lieu 2002: 31–68). This may be one reason why there was no systematic attempt to eliminate Christians before the mid-third century. Nevertheless, for three centuries Christians were at risk. The risk was statistically small, but they could be executed, sometimes with appalling but entirely legal cruelty, for their refusal to worship the gods of the empire. Roman law imposed a particular form of martyrdom, that is, dying for one's beliefs, that became part of Christian self-understanding, and was commemorated as the church's history of heroism (ch. 3).

In the early fourth century, the Roman emperor Constantine ended this danger and gave the Christian church his official support and funding (ch. 6). Thereafter, emperors were involved in debates about which Christians were orthodox (ch. 2) and deserved their support. Constantine also gave Christian bishops (Greek *episkopos*, 'supervisor') a recognised role in local administration of law. The church became an alternative career for people who could otherwise have entered the imperial service, and the pastoral work of a bishop, as leader of a church community, came to include the settlement of legal disputes and negotiation with civic and imperial authorities. Christian concern for the poor prompted building programmes, administrative systems, and legislation on charitable bequests and institutions. Church buildings, and church organisation, show how Roman civic culture contributed to the vocabulary and the practices of the church. Early Christian groups met in private houses, and no church building earlier than the mid-third century has yet been identified (White 1990). Many of the church buildings funded by Constantine, and by other fourth-century Christian patrons, were basilicas, large rectangular halls with a platform at one end. This was the all-purpose official building: 'basilica' means literally 'royal', from Greek *basilikos*. The emperor or his deputy presided in a basilica that was a courtroom, for policy-making or for trials. The bishop or his deputy presided in a church; a professor or his deputy presided in a lecture-room. Emperor, bishop or professor sat in a high-backed chair, *cathedra*, on the raised platform. (That is why professors have chairs, and why some churches are cathedrals.) The bishop taught his congregation like a professor (ch. 5), and took responsibility for his diocese, another term from Roman administration: *dioikēsis* is Greek for an administrative region. Similarly, 'parish' comes from Greek *paroikia*, 'neighbourhood', and 'vicar' from Latin *vicarius*, 'deputy'.

The values of Roman civic culture shaped the lives even of those Christians, known as ascetics (from Greek *askēsis*, 'training'), who expressed their total commitment to God by rejecting those values and devoting themselves to an austere life of prayer and study of the Bible. Their form of asceticism was influenced by philosophical teaching (ch. 4). Educated Christian preachers used the traditions of classical philosophy and literature to interpret the Christian scriptures (ch. 5). By the late fourth century Roman law had established Christianity as the authorised religion of the empire, and people who were classified as pagans, Jews and heretics came under increasing pressure to conform (ch. 6). In the western half of the Roman empire, when imperial government collapsed in the late fifth century, it was the church that preserved and transmitted Latin language and literature, Graeco-Roman philosophical theology, and Roman administrative structures.

No wonder, then, that many Christian writers in the early centuries CE interpreted the Roman empire as part of God's purpose for the world (Markus 1988: 47–51). Jesus Christ was born in the reign of Augustus, who united the Roman empire. The territory controlled by Rome, at its greatest extent, stretched from Scotland to the Sudan and from Spain to Mesopotamia. This was the biggest and the longest-lasting empire known to western history, and it shaped the later history of Europe and the Mediterranean world. Two thousand years after the birth of Christ, Christian texts, theology, organisation and ritual are still bearers of Roman tradition, and the church powerfully influenced the way in which Roman tradition was transmitted to post-Roman cultures. Many Christians still regard as authoritative the decisions and interpretations and belief-statements made by Christians who lived in the Roman empire. In the late twentieth and early twenty-first centuries, this has been most obvious in debates on questions of gender and sexuality: whether women can be validly ordained as priests, whether priests must be celibate, whether extra-marital relationships are wrong, whether homosexual relationships are wrong (ch. 4). There are also debates about the content of the creeds (Latin *credo*, 'I believe'), the statements of Christian belief that were formulated in the fourth and fifth centuries (Young 1983, Wickham 1997). Two church councils, Nicaea (325) and Chalcedon (451) were especially influential in this process, but there was strong dissent from both. Moreover, their discussion was framed by the philosophical debates of the time, and many present-day theologians find this unhelpful. For non-Christian students of Roman history, and indeed for some Christians, early Christian theology and practice can be very puzzling. This is a historian's, not a theologian's, book, but historical context can often help to explain.

DIFFERENCES

Christians did not share in Roman religious practice, because they thought that Romans worshipped idols, images of false or even demonic gods. Greek has two words for images, with different implications. 'Idol' comes from Greek *eidōlon*, which usually means a deceptive or shadowy image of reality, like the shades in Homer's account of the Underworld. 'Icon', a religious image, comes from *eikōn*, 'likeness': some philosophers argued that an *eikōn* can be a likeness of reality, and some suggested that the gods were willing to inhabit an image that was made with reverence. Christians borrowed from philosophical critique of image-making to argue that cult-statues were idols: either they were nothing more than wood and stone, or, if they had power, it was the power of the demons who had taken up residence there, attracted by the blood of animal sacrifice. Christians of course refused to sacrifice to idols; they also rejected Jewish sacrifice, because they interpreted the death of Christ as the perfect sacrifice and commemorated it in the central Christian ritual of the eucharist (ch. 2).

Christians also borrowed from philosophy to interpret their sacred texts, that is, the Jewish scriptures, together with a range of first-century Christian texts that came to be regarded as authoritative (ch. 5). Roman culture had many sacred texts, but none had a comparable role in shaping belief and practice (ch. 2, ch. 5). The Christian texts acquired the name 'New Testament' from a letter written by the Christian missionary Paul of Tarsus, formerly a strictly observant Jew (ch. 2), in the mid-first century. Paul said (2 Corinthians 3.6) that God had made a new agreement (Greek *diathēkē*) with his people. This word, which also means 'will' or 'disposition of property', was translated into Latin as *testamentum*. By the second century, if not sooner, Christians were calling Jewish scripture the Old Testament; many present-day theologians prefer to say 'Hebrew Bible', without the implication that Jewish scripture is outdated. The New Testament texts come from the first or, at the latest, the early second century. They show Jews varying in their assimilation to local cultures, and Christians varying in the extent to which they maintained or adopted Jewish practices, and in the extent to which they shared the culture and customs of the Roman empire.

These same texts often make sharp contrasts, between Christians and Jews and between Christians and 'Gentiles' or 'Greeks'. 'Gentile' is the Latin equivalent of Hebrew *goyim* (plural of the more familiar *goy*), 'the peoples' or 'the nations' who are not Jews. The Greek word for 'people' in this sense is *ethnos*, with the adjective *ethnikos* (cf. 'ethnic'); the Latin equivalent is *gens* with the adjective *gentilis*, hence 'Gentile'. Jews and Christians in Greek-speaking regions often referred to non-believers as 'the Greeks', even though they themselves spoke Greek. This raises interesting, and topical, questions about cultural identity: is it possible to share language and culture without sharing religion (ch. 5)? In the last half-century, social and religious change has prompted reassessment of the clear contrasts that are affirmed in early Christian texts and maintained in the pioneering church history of Eusebius.

Eusebius, bishop of Caesarea in Palestine, began his *History of the Church* in the early fourth century, when Christians were undergoing the worst persecution they had ever known. His teacher Pamphilus, who died in this persecution, was a student of the great (and controversial) theologian

Origen, who died as a result of torture and imprisonment in the mid-
third century (ch. 3). Eusebius too lived through atrocious persecution: his
account of the martyrs of Palestine is among the most horrific in a horrific
genre. He survived to see the transformation of his world by Constantine's
support for Christianity.[5] He began his history as follows:

> My aim is to record in writing: the successions of the holy apostles, from our Saviour
> to our own times; what was done and when in the history of the church; its most
> distinguished leaders in the best-known regions; those who, in each generation,
> spread God's word in writing or without; and the names, number and age of those
> who, driven to the utmost error by their desire for innovation, have proclaimed
> themselves the bringers of so-called knowledge, and have set upon Christ's flock
> like savage wolves. Also: what has happened to the Jews from the moment of their
> conspiracy against our Saviour; what wars the gentiles fought, and when, against
> God's word; the martyrdoms of our own times; and our Saviour's gracious help
> in all.

Eusebius saw a continuous Christian tradition, exemplified by the transmission of authority from apostles to a succession of bishops,[6] and growing
steadily from the earliest churches and missions. The tradition that he saw
was clearly distinct from Judaism. It survived three centuries of state persecution, and even more dangerous internal threat from heretics. At last,
in Eusebius' final book, Constantine ends persecution and Christianity
becomes the dominant religion of the Roman empire.

This was Christian history written by the victors, who knew the tri-
umphant end of the story. In later centuries, historians who followed the
example of Eusebius focussed on the Church's own history within Roman
society, and on its internal debates about doctrine and practice and organisation. They could assume readers who were Christians or who at least took
a sympathetic interest in Christianity, and their attitude to other religions
now provokes an amazement that shows how radically church history has
changed (J. Lieu 2002: 69–70). Often they wrote with the aim of demon-
strating that a particular Christian tradition was (the only one) true to the
earliest churches. 'Church history' was thus separated from 'Roman history', which dealt with war and politics, though Roman historians would
probably include a chapter on the rise of Christianity, and church historians

---

[5] On Eusebius, see T. Barnes 1981, Cameron and Hall 1999. His *Ecclesiastical History* is translated by
Williamson 1989; and by Lawlor and Oulton 1927, with notes.

[6] Apostles (Greek *apostolos*, 'envoy') were the first Christian missionaries, commissioned (according to
the Gospels) by Jesus himself. A bishop was the head of a church and later of a group of churches,
appointed for life.

would probably include a chapter on the political and social structures of the Roman empire.

Some histories of the church were hostile to Christianity, usually in reaction to the writer's own experience of Christian teaching and practice. These also accepted the framework of Eusebius, but presented Christianity as an example of human credulity or, worse, of human readiness to invent and accept systems of oppression. Thus Edward Gibbon, in *Decline and Fall of the Roman Empire* (published 1776–88), saw 'religion' as a cause of decline from the high point of human happiness in the civilised cities of the mid-second century, and ascribed the fall of the Roman empire to 'barbarism and religion' (ch. 71). In more recent scholarship, Christianity has been blamed for diverting financial and human resources from the classical city; for inflicting, as soon as it had the chance, terrible harm on those it classed as Jews, infidels or heretics; and for stamping sexual guilt and repressive morality into the culture that Europeans exported throughout the world (ch. 4, ch. 6).

In the later twentieth century, historians became much less willing to accept the 'grand narrative' of the Christianisation of the Roman world. One factor in this was a general rejection of teleological narratives (that is, narratives shaped by their *telos* or goal) in favour of different plot-lines: religious diversity, multiplicity, and rejection of closure (that is, reluctance to identify a decisive end of the story). Historians have always attended to the rhetoric and the agenda of their sources: the 'literary turn' in historical studies made them give special attention to the representation and construction of different groups (for example, women, men, Jews, Christians, pagans, Romans, heretics, orthodox), and to the presuppositions implicit in their own way of writing. These trends in historical writing combined with social factors. Formal church membership and attendance declined, many theologians and religious believers engaged in dialogue with other religious traditions, and Britain, once consciously Christian, became consciously pluralist and multicultural. From the late 1960s on, European and North American historians were very interested in the multicultural society of late antiquity, that is, the Roman empire in (approximately) the third to the sixth centuries. Several recent surveys reflect these pluralist concerns: *Religions of Rome* (Beard–North–Price 1998), *Religions of the Ancient Greeks* (Price 1999), *Religions of Late Antiquity in Practice* (Valantasis 2000), *Readings in Late Antiquity* (Maas 2000). Another 'grand narrative' was abandoned when late antiquity was no longer seen as a decline and fall from classical perfection, the collapse of a great empire undermined by Christianity and assaulted by barbarians, but as the gradual transformation of the classical heritage in response to other cultures (Vessey 1998).

There are many perspectives on late antiquity, but its historians recognise that Roman history and Christian history are not separate. Present-day historians are not likely to argue for the truth or untruth of religious claims: rather, they differ in that some historians think that some people have religious motives, others think that religious motives consciously or unconsciously hide personal or political concerns (ch. 4, ch. 6). Present-day theologians are likely to interpret early Christian writings in relation to specific cultural contexts, rather than looking for a sequence (formerly called a *catena*, 'chain') of timeless truths beginning with the Fathers of the Church. The Fathers (Latin *patres*, hence 'patristics') are the authoritative writers of the early Church, most of whom wrote in Greek or Latin, and all of whom were men (ch. 2). Historians of late antiquity, and sociologists of religion, are interested in the varieties of human behaviour and the operation of religious movements in different societies. For example, the sociologist Rodney Stark (1996) consciously 'visited' early Christianity with models derived from the study of recent religious movements, and historians and theologians responded (Castelli 1998) with the detail, and the aspects of ancient 'mentality', that do not fit the models. The historian Hal Drake consciously interprets Constantine in terms of current political theory and practice: 'this is a book about politics' (Drake 2000: xv).

As religious fundamentalism became a political force in several cultures, theologians and sociologists have tried to explain why people are willing to believe in the absolute authority of a sacred text, of a tradition of interpretation, and of charismatic or inherited religious leadership. Historians have considered how much Judaism, Christianity and Islam, the three 'religions of the book', have in common, and to what extent each was shaped by the culture of the Roman empire and its continuators, the successor-kingdoms in western Europe and the Byzantine empire in the eastern Mediterranean. Serious theological dialogue between Christians and Jews, and serious efforts to challenge anti-semitism, followed the horrors of the Holocaust (Fredriksen and Reinhartz 2002). Dialogue with Islam has taken longer, not least because far fewer western scholars understand the traditions and the languages.[7] But present-day western Christians can see similarities to their own early relationship with Roman society (ch. 2) in the range of Muslim attitudes to western society and to the fighters whom

---

[7] Early Islam in relation to late antiquity: Bowersock 1990; Fowden 1993; Kennedy 1999; C. Robinson 1999, 2003; Louth 2002.

some, but not all, Muslims call martyrs (ch. 3). They can also see similarities when western Muslims face accusations that they are not part of the
societies in which they live, or, worse, that Islam preaches holy war and
'Islamic' equals 'terrorist'; and when Muslims reply by pointing to Islamic
teachings on peace and to their own strong social ethics.

Any book on Christianity and Roman society, whatever its perspective,
must still confront the great question: how on earth did this tiny religious
splinter-group survive to become the dominant religion of the Roman
world? Confident Christian authors still reply, as they did in the early centuries, that there is only one possible explanation for this extraordinary fact.
Christianity, they say, is true, and its truth prevailed over the outworn or
inadequate religions of the Roman world. Christians proclaimed a loving
God who created humanity and who took the initiative, through the life
and teachings of Jesus, to reconcile God with an alienated humanity that
had resisted the efforts of philosophers and prophets. Christians overcame
the constraints of gender roles, ethnicity, social status and education: they
offered everyone who was willing to listen the assurance of God's love, clear
ethical and religious teaching, and a supportive community. Thus Christianity grew despite persecution; or rather, persecution helped it to grow,
because the deaths of martyrs were the ultimate proof of faith. The Christian churches took responsibility for helping those in need and teaching
all who would listen, and were ready to respond to Constantine's support
by increasing their outreach. Christian teaching and practice transformed
Roman society.

Confident anti-Christian authors still reply, as they did in the early centuries, that Christianity traded on credulity and fear. The early Roman
empire was a supermarket of religions, and the Christian special offer was
free physical healing and spiritual salvation. It appealed, as cults will always
appeal, to the ignorant and vulnerable, those who knew no better. Christian
leaders frightened or flattered the rich into diverting their resources from
family and city to the church, and used those resources to rival the traditional civic patrons. They encouraged fanatics to seek a martyr's death, or
to renounce marriage and family duty for the self-inflicted starvation and
repression of extreme asceticism. They diverted attention from present
suffering to happiness in heaven. The eventual success of Christianity
depended on the personal credulity of Constantine; or on his need for
a support-base and a pulpit; or on the Roman empire's need for a unifying
religion, since the Sassanid rulers of Persia had used the Zoroastrian religion to unite Rome's most dangerous opponent. Once Constantine had
provided the funding, a church career offered rewards that attracted able

people away from the service of the empire. Most people prudently said they were Christian, but went on living much as they had done before. Comparative sociology shows how Christianity survived and spread by the classic technique of cells linked by networks, then made itself acceptable by interpreting unfamiliar Jewish scripture through familiar Greek philosophy and by teaching ethics that were already the norm for decent Roman citizens. Christianity was parasitic on Roman society.

So who is right? Recent scholarship emphasises the diversity of both Roman and Christian traditions, rather than the differences between them. One reason for this change is cultural and religious pluralism, another is more obviously academic: scholars have learned about diversity through interdisciplinary work on the complex Roman world in which Christianity developed. The study of late antiquity needs classicists and medievalists, historians and art historians, anthropologists and archaeologists, theologians and legal historians, papyrologists and epigraphers. It needs specialists in regional cultures who know Syriac and Coptic and Ethiopic, classical Armenian and Georgian; Judaists who can follow the elliptical and ironic arguments used in late-antique Jewish debate; experts in classical Arabic and early Islam. The rise of late antiquity as a field of study has been greatly helped by the sharing of expertise on the internet.

Older books, in the tradition of Eusebius, often had introductory chapters on 'Christianity and its pagan background' and 'Christianity and its Jewish background'. Christianity was the star performer, instantly recognisable, in front of a static backdrop painted with a broad brush. That has changed, because there is much more information on the diversity of religions, their regional and cultural contexts, and change over time. One sign of change is the widespread use of CE (Common Era) and BCE (Before Common Era) rather than AD (*Anno Domini*, 'in the year of the Lord') and BC (Before Christ). More generally, scholars prefer to talk in terms of diversity and pluralism, shifting frontiers and blurred boundaries. They avoid the traditional distinctions between orthodox Christians and heretics, Jews and Christians, pagans and Christians, and they suspect any broad generalisations about what these people believed or did in the name of religion. It used to be widely accepted that Christianity succeeded because traditional Roman religion was a system of impersonal civic cults that failed to meet the moral and spiritual needs of individuals, and because Judaism, which did meet moral and spiritual needs, was exclusive and rule-governed. But the current consensus is that both these characterisations are much too limited. The first and second centuries CE saw a general trend towards belief in one supreme god (ch. 5) and in the survival of the soul after death, ethical teaching, and attention to texts that were thought to reveal religious truths. Judaism was exclusive for insiders, but inclusive for outsiders (Fredriksen and Reinhartz 2002: 14). The Roman world offered many charismatic religious leaders and elective cults, and people could follow them without rejecting local religious custom (Liebeschuetz 2000).

So if Christianity was one among many religious options in Roman society, proclaiming one among many saviours, why would anybody choose it? This was the one option that was neither compatible with traditional religion, nor respected as Judaism was for its ancient monotheist tradition. Instead, its followers were expected to refuse to sacrifice, to deny the divinity of the gods who made Rome great, and to affirm instead the exclusive divinity of a man who had been sentenced by Roman law to death on a cross. The traditional Christian answer uses words ascribed to the Jewish teacher Gamaliel. 'If this enterprise, this movement of theirs, is of human origin, it will break up of its own accord; but if it does in fact come from God, you will not only be unable to destroy them, but you might find yourselves fighting against God' (Acts 5.38–9). But even for those who think that explains why Christianity survived, there is still a question how.

CHAPTER 2

Christians and others

The story of the cross is foolishness to the lost, but to us, who are saved, it is the power of God. Scripture says, 'I shall destroy the wisdom of the wise, and bring to nothing the learning of the learned.' Where is the wise man now? Where is the scribe? Where is the investigator of this present age? Has not God made the wisdom of the world look foolish? Through God's wisdom the world did not know God through its own wisdom, and God saw fit to save believers by the foolishness of our preaching. Jews ask for signs, Greeks look for wisdom, but we preach Christ crucified, an obstacle to the Jews and foolishness to the Gentiles, but to those who are called, both Jews and Greeks, Christ the power and the wisdom of God. For the foolishness of God is wiser than human beings, and the weakness of God is stronger.

(Paul of Tarsus, 1 Corinthians 1.18–25; mid-first century)

Victorinus, so Simplicianus said, read Holy Scripture and all kinds of Christian literature with the most careful attention. He used to say to Simplicianus, not openly but in private conversation, 'You should know that I am already a Christian.' Simplicianus would reply, 'I shall not believe it, or count you as a Christian, unless I see you in Christ's church.' Victorinus would laugh at him and say, 'So walls make Christians?'

(Augustine, *Confessions* 8.2.4, written c. 395; this story dates from the 350s)

ROMANS ON CHRISTIANS

For Christianity to succeed in the Roman world, it had to persuade those who were not Christians to join or at least to tolerate it. But what did those others think about Christianity? Almost all the written evidence comes from a Christian perspective. This is a familiar problem for students of ancient history: we have Herodotus on Persians, Thucydides on Spartans, Tacitus on Germans, not what Persians or Spartans or Germans thought about the peoples who defeated them. But the case of Christianity is rather different. Thucydides and Tacitus wrote speeches to present arguments against the imperialism of their own countries, but Christian writers had no reason to present arguments for religions they thought dangerously wrong. There were some anti-Christian writings, but they may not have been widely circulated, and Christian copyists had no reason to transmit them to later ages. Consequently, we do not have a complete text of Celsus, *The True Account* (c. 175), which attacked Christians for abandoning the common religious heritage in favour of a garbled 'barbarian', that is, non-Greek, version (ch. 5), and not even doing that properly, since they also rebelled against Judaism. Very little survives of Hierocles, *The Friend of Truth* (c. 300), which argued that Jesus Christ was outclassed by the first-century philosopher and wonder-worker Apollonius of Tyana. Longer, but still incomplete, extracts survive from *Against the Galilaeans* by the emperor Julian 'the apostate' (c. 360), who renounced the Christianity in which he was brought up. 'Galilaeans' was Julian's name for Christians: he wanted to contrast Christianity, which began in the obscure provincial district of Galilee, with the ancient Hellenic tradition. We know about these anti-Christian texts because they were quoted (selectively) and paraphrased (tendentiously) by Christian authors: Origen, *Against Celsus* (*Contra Celsum*), Eusebius, *Against Hierocles*, and Cyril of Alexandria, *Against Julian*. The most spectacular example of the lost opposition is the third-century philosopher Porphyry, whose books were publicly burned, allegedly on the orders of Constantine, because of his fierce opposition to Christianity (ch. 3). Porphyry is credited with about seventy books, including fifteen (perhaps part of a longer work) against Christians. Little remains from this output, and most of the fragments of Porphyry survived because Christian authors, chiefly Eusebius and Augustine, used them as ammunition.[1]

We do not know whether there were many other texts, now lost, that challenged or attacked Christianity. It depends how soon, and how generally, Christianity was seen as a serious threat to Roman religion and society (ch. 3), and that in turn depends on some unanswerable questions about the distinctiveness of Christianity, and the number of Christians, in the centuries before Constantine (see below). In the first and second centuries, several Christians wrote in defence of their religion. These writings are called 'apologetic', from Greek *apologia*, 'speech for the defence',

---

[1] Wilken 2003 interprets pagan critique of Christianity as serious dialogue. Porphyry: brief introduction G. Clark 2000a: 5–6; extensive discussion Digeser 2000. Hierocles: Hagg 1992 argues that this Eusebius is not the church historian; see further ch. 3 for Lactantius on philosophic attacks. Origen against Celsus: tr. Chadwick 1965; Frede 1999. Julian, *Against the Galilaeans*: R. Smith 1995, and on Cyril, Wilken 1999.

but it is not clear that the defence responded to attack (Edwards et al. 1999). Romans affirmed the common religious tradition derived from the gods (Boys-Stones 2001), but saw no need to present their case in detail; if there were Jewish challenges to Christianity, they do not survive (Goodman 1999).

One well-known group of texts does present Roman perspectives on Christians in the first and early second centuries, but only as one, minor, concern among many others. The authors, Suetonius, Tacitus and Pliny, knew each other well enough to count as friends. Suetonius, a bureaucrat in the service of the emperor Hadrian (early second century), wrote *Lives* of the first twelve Caesars. In his life of Claudius (25.4) he mentioned the expulsion of Jews from Rome, around 49 CE, because of disturbances 'prompted by Chrestus': this may or may not refer to disputes in the Jewish community caused by Christian teaching. He also mentioned the execution of Christians, in a list of 'clean up Rome' measures taken by Nero in his early, virtuous days:

Conspicuous consumption was limited. Public dinners were limited to food-baskets. Food-shops were forbidden to sell any cooked food other than pulses and vegetables, whereas previously they had offered every kind of snack. Christians, who were followers of a new and wicked cult (*superstitio nova ac malefica*), were put to death. Charioteer rags were banned: it had become accepted that they could go where they pleased, playing tricks and behaving like hooligans. Stage stars (*pantomimi*) and their claques were sent away from Rome. (Suetonius, *Life of Nero* 16.2)

The historian Tacitus, governor of the province of Asia under Hadrian's predecessor Trajan, went into more detail about the execution of Christians who were scapegoated by Nero for the fire that in 64 destroyed large areas of Rome.

They were those commonly known as Christiani and hated for their crimes (*flagitia*). The name came from Christus, who was executed by the procurator Pontius Pilatus in the reign of Tiberius. The pernicious cult (*exitiabilis superstitio*) was suppressed at the time, but was breaking out again, not only in Judaea, the source of the evil, but also in Rome, where all disgraceful or shameful practices convene from all directions to be followed. So first those who admitted it were arrested, then on their evidence a great multitude of others were convicted not so much on the charge of arson as for hatred of the human race. (Tacitus, *Annals* 15.44)

Superstitio applies to practices that Romans did not count as acceptable religion (Beard–North–Price 1998: 1.217–27). Suetonius and Tacitus characterise Christian *superstitio* as pernicious, and that reaction corresponds to the deaths inflicted on Christians in 64. The 'extreme penalties' of Roman law included burning alive and exposure to wild animals in the arena. Nero's artistic variations on the theme (Coleman 1990) included using Christians as live torches, to fit the crime of arson; and dressing them in the skins of beasts, so that they entered the arena not as criminal humans who had to face wild animals, but as wild beasts who were hunted with dogs.

The third of these three friends, the younger Pliny (so called to distinguish him from his uncle who wrote the *Natural History*), was sent, c. 112 CE, as special envoy of Trajan to deal with corruption in Bithynia, a Roman province in northern Asia Minor. Book 10 of Pliny's collected letters consists of official correspondence, and was probably intended as a model of imperial paper trails. One of the many questions on which Pliny consulted Trajan (*Ep.* 10.96) was what to do with people denounced as Christians. He had no previous experience of judicial enquiry (*cognitio*) concerned with Christians, so he did not know whether he should be lenient to people who were no longer Christian, and whether he should punish only for 'the name' when there was no evidence of wrongdoing. He used investigative torture on two slave-women, but found only a 'perverse and excessive superstition' (*superstitio prava et immodica*). Christians met before dawn to sing a hymn to Christ as God, and took an oath to behave well. Then they dispersed, and met again, after the working day, for an ordinary meal; but they had stopped doing this after Pliny issued an edict banning unauthorised meetings. Two other letters (10.33–4) provide a context for the ban. Trajan refused a request to establish a fire brigade in Nicomedia, because 'whatever name we give them, for whatever reason, men brought together for a common purpose quickly become a *hetairia*'. *Hetairia* is Greek for a political association.

Trajan confirmed (10.97) the action that Pliny had taken: leniency for those who proved, by cursing Christ and venerating the emperor's image, that they were not now Christian; punishment for those who persisted in refusing the demand of a Roman official; no anonymous denunciations to be accepted. But he could have taken this episode much more seriously. Celsus (Origen, *Contra Celsum* 8.17) said that the absence of altars and images and temples in Christian worship was a sure sign of a secret society. Romans expected conspirators to meet under cover of darkness (like the fire brigade?) and to share oaths and food, or even to commit a human sacrifice so that they were bound by shared crime (cf. Sallust, *Bellum Catilinae* 22.1–2, Rives 1995). Christian ritual and belief could easily have been misinterpreted as conspiracy. Jesus, at his last meal with his followers, interpreted the Passover bread and wine as his own body and blood given for them (Matthew 26.26–8); commemoration of this meal became the central Christian ritual (1 Corinthians 11.23–7), the eucharist

(Greek *eucharistia*, 'thanksgiving'), also known as 'communion'. Romans also expected conspirators to destroy the social order if they could. Rome's exceptional political and military success was ascribed to its reverence for the gods, so those who rejected Roman religion were obviously anti-social conspirators, whose neglect of the gods prompted divine vengeance. Some Christians confirmed this perception by declaring that Roman society was oppressive and idolatrous, and that the world would soon end amid consuming fire. 'Apocalypse', now used to mean the end of the world or the collapse of civilisation, derives from Greek *apokalupsis*, 'revelation'. The book of Revelation, which after much debate was included in the canon (see ch. 5) of the New Testament, proclaims the downfall of Babylon the Great, the Woman in Scarlet 'with whom all the kings of the earth have committed fornication' (Revelation 17.2). This imagery from Jewish scripture symbolises Rome.[2]

Romans, then, might regard Christians as dangers to society, potential arsonists, or, if nothing worse, subverters of household loyalties (Benko 1984, Wilken 2003). New religious cults notoriously gave outsiders a route into households, especially through women (Plutarch, *Moralia* 140d; Beard–North–Price 1998: 1.297–300), and here too Christian language was open to misunderstanding. Cannibalism and incest were the markers of the anti-social Other (Rives 1995). Christians not only shared a meal that they interpreted as flesh and blood, they were encouraged to call each other 'brother' and 'sister' and their elders 'father', and to greet one another with the kiss that symbolised a family tie or a recognised social bond (Penn 2002). Wild stories circulated, and outsiders were suspicious, especially when it was Christians who told these stories about other Christians (Wilken 2003: 19–21; see below).

Christian organisation might also reinforce suspicions of a world-wide conspiracy, for early Christian groups had a classic 'cell and network' strategy for cohesion and growth.[3] Paul's letter to the church at Corinth exemplifies it:

All the churches of Asia [the Roman province, Asia Minor] send you greetings. Aquila and Prisca, with the church that meets at their house, send you their warmest wishes, in the Lord. All the brothers send you their greetings. Greet one another with a holy kiss. (1 Corinthians 16.19–20)

---

[2] Revelation supplies many familiar phrases: 'the Scarlet Woman', 'the mark of the beast', 'the New Jerusalem', and Babylon as the image of a corrupt and doomed society. On apocalyptic in the early centuries CE, see Rowland 1985: 56–64; Potter 1990.

[3] For comparative sociology applied to early Christian groups, see e.g. Meeks 1983, Esler 1994, Stark 1996, Moxnes 1997.

A Christian church called itself an 'assembly' (*ekklēsia*), a political term that might suggest an alternative society; but it functioned like an alternative family, offering spiritual and practical support.[4] Often a church began in a household, when the head of household was baptised as a Christian and the other members, including the slaves, followed his or her example. As the church grew, it was like an extended household, meeting in a private house and using family language: brothers, sisters, fathers (but not mothers, see below). Its most important ritual was a shared meal, varying in content, but different from Graeco-Roman ceremonial meals in that it did not centre on animal sacrifice (McGowan 1999). Its members met regularly, perhaps daily like the Christians Pliny found in Bithynia, perhaps weekly in association with local Jewish groups (see below). Christian networks allowed members of these cells to feel that they were part of a world-wide movement that was similar in local structures and connected by exchanges of letters, by a shared sacred text, and by discussions of belief and practice. According to early Christian texts, a Christian could travel the length of the Mediterranean, taking a letter of commendation from the local church, and find hospitality and practical help from any other church.

The contrast between Christian groups and other voluntary associations may have been overstated (Ascough 1997); philosophical groups also had close bonds, and their members intermarried (Fowden 1982); and it is particularly difficult (see below) to distinguish Christian from Jewish communities. But there is no clear evidence (see below) that other associations provided comparable support and comparable networking for their members. Those on the outside might react to Christian cells as the Roman government in the third century reacted to Manichaean cells (ch. 3), or as western governments in the 1950s reacted to Communist cells, or as most people react now to religious movements that they regard as cults. Christian groups could be thought to subvert family and society by placing loyalty to the group leaders and their teachings above other ties; to prey on those who were emotionally vulnerable and easily brainwashed; and to be centres of terrorist conspiracy.

A BETTER OFFER?

Were Christian churches unique in their cohesion and in the support that they offered their members? Here again there is a problem of sources. Early

---

[4] *ekklēsia* (via Latin) gives French 'église' and Spanish 'iglesia'. 'Church', and German 'Kirche', come from the adjective *kuriakē*, 'of the Lord'.

Christian texts, especially the letters of Paul of Tarsus (mid-first century), describe Christian communities and networks in some detail, and acknowledge problems as well as presenting ideals. There are no comparable Roman sources for the 'elective' religious groups that had practices in common with Christian groups. Civic cults typically had an annual festival, but many elective groups met regularly, perhaps once a month, for a celebratory meal in honour of their patron deity. (Jews were unusual in making every seventh day holy, and some Romans thought the Jewish Sabbath was an excuse for idleness.) Some groups provided mutual support for members, often in the form of a funeral fund (Wilken 2003: 14–15). They had rules, and in at least one such group, the rules included moral behaviour (Barton and Horsley 1981). A group called 'Christiani' (Acts 11.26) would initially have seemed like 'Heraklistai' or 'Asklepiastai' (Wilken 2003: 44), worshippers of a god who, like Herakles and Asklepios, had once been mortal.

So several elements of Christian practice can be paralleled in other cults, but there are some distinctive features. One is the shared sacred text. Many groups had texts, some secret, some public, that they considered sacred: for instance, 'Orphic' groups had poems ascribed to the legendary sage and poet Orpheus. None, so far as we know, had texts as extensive or as consistently used as the scriptures shared by Jews and Christians (Gamble 1995; see below, ch. 5). Moreover, if there were people who gave authoritative readings of other sacred texts, such people are not known to have represented their groups in a Mediterranean-wide network, as Christian bishops represented their churches. New Testament texts show Christian groups exchanging news and greetings, comparing notes on belief and practice and on the interpretation of the scriptures, and collecting money to help fellow-Christians. As always, it is difficult to distinguish Christian practice from Jewish (see below), but there is nothing comparable in Roman religion, either in civic or in elective cults. For example, Apollonius of Tyana was presented as a rival to Christ (Swain 1997), but Philostratus, *In Honour of Apollonius* (c. 230) does not suggest that his admirers in Rome were in touch with admirers in Alexandria. Similarly, there were many groups called 'worshippers of Dionysus', but there is no evidence that they made connections, exchanged their sacred texts, or tried to maintain consistency of belief and practice (Turcan 1996: 291–300).

Pythagoreans were perhaps an exception. According to their tradition, followers of the archaic sage Pythagoras had in common his secret teachings, which were revealed only after a long initiation; they recognised each other by secret tokens (*sumbolon*, see ch. 5) and were committed to give any other Pythagorean all the help that was in their power. But very few people counted themselves as Pythagorean, and the tradition is full of problems because stories of Pythagoras and his followers were set in a distant past, and many of the writings ascribed to him were denounced as forgeries. The fullest account of Pythagorean lifestyle comes from the late third century CE. This is *On the Pythagorean Life*, by the philosopher Iamblichus, who made use of earlier sources but had his own agenda for the philosophic life (ch. 4) and may have intended a challenge to Christianity (but see G. Clark 2000b).

There is textual and material evidence that some elective cults spread across the Mediterranean world, maintaining similar hierarchies and practices in different regions. Initiates of Mithras, who were identified by a *sumbolon* of their rank, were likely to find a Mithraeum wherever they travelled; but this cult almost certainly excluded women (G. Clark 2000a: 188 n. 637). Worshippers of Isis might find a conspicuous Isis-temple; but there is a question whether an initiate could arrive in a new place and immediately join a group (Beard–North–Price 1998: 1.302–4). The second-century novel by Apuleius, *Metamorphoses* (also called *The Golden Ass*), shows the hero paying to undergo successive initiations in different places, and there is much debate on whether Apuleius shows genuine devotion to Isis, or whether his naïve hero really is a golden ass exploited by greedy Isis-priests (S. J. Harrison 2000).

It is also not clear that such elective cults offered a supportive community of worshippers. Another distinctive feature of Christian groups is the requirement to help those in need:

'Lord, when did we see you hungry and feed you, or thirsty and give you drink? When did we see you a stranger and make you welcome; naked and clothe you; sick or in prison and go to see you?' And the King will answer, 'I tell you solemnly, in so far as you did it to one of the least of these brothers of mine, you did it to me.' (Matthew 25.38–40)

No Roman cult groups, not even those that were primarily mutual support groups, are known to have looked after strangers and people in need. In the mid-fourth century, the emperor Julian commented (*Epistles* 84) that Jews and Christians provided not only for their own poor, but also for the poor of the Hellenes, his preferred term for followers of the traditional religion (ch. 5). Civic religion did not exclude the poor, and philosophers said that the simple offerings of the poor, given in piety, were more pleasing to the gods than the most lavish offerings (Porphyry, *De Abstinentia* 2.16, quoting Theophrastus). But when philosophers debated whether the gods want sacrifice, they did not use the argument that the gods approved of sacrifice because it provided food or instruction. Provision for the poor was not an ethical priority in Roman culture (ch. 6), whereas Christians were expected to take the gospel to the poor and to help those in need. It is difficult to show that most Christian converts were poor (see below), either in the sense that they were not rich or in the sense that they were actually destitute; but practical help for those who needed it may have been an important factor in the growth of Christianity. For example, Eusebius (*Ecclesiastical History* 7.22.7–10) cites a letter of Dionysius, bishop of Alexandria in the mid-third century, on how Christians nursed plague victims and gave them burial, regardless of the danger, while pagans abandoned even family members. Nursing care would improve the survival rate, and that might convince others that Christians had special religious protection; beliefs that make sense of suffering can also affect survival rates (Stark 1996: 73–94). Hope of salvation (Greek *sōtēria*, literally 'safety') in this life and after, and stories of miraculous healing and protection, may have had more effect than any exposition of Christian doctrine (MacMullen 1984).

Christianity, then, offered a distinctive and effective combination of shared ethics and sacred text, a supportive community with outreach to those in need, regular meetings and Mediterranean-wide connections. Was this also distinctive within Judaism? There is surprisingly little evidence, textual or material, to show how Judaism of the early centuries CE varied in specific contexts (Rowland 1985: 313–27 for texts; Rajak 2001). There were, and are, many different interpretations of Jewish belief and practice. Some scholars express this complexity by referring to 'Judaisms' in the plural. Others prefer the singular, because they see a common core or, more likely, a set of family resemblances in a religion that was 'complex, capacious and rather frayed at the edges' (Schwartz 2001: 9). The problem in identifying variations over time and place is that there was a continuous tradition of Jewish teaching and debate on the Torah (the law) ascribed to Moses. After the Romans destroyed the Jerusalem Temple, the centre of Jewish sacrificial worship, in 70 CE, these debates became even more important. The label 'rabbinic Judaism', often used for this post-Temple period, comes from the honorific title 'rabbi', 'my teacher'. The great collections of rabbinic discussion assemble material from different periods and places, some of them from the regions that Jews called Babylon, beyond the river Euphrates and outside the Roman empire. The Mishnah probably reflects the state of debate in second-century Palestine; the Babylonian and the Palestinian Talmud may have been compiled as late as the sixth century. This is a tradition that expects differences of opinion and unresolved debates (Boyarin 1999), and it is difficult to provide a context for any reported opinion or practice. One example of the problem is a notorious assertion that Jews curse Christ in their synagogues. This accusation comes from the second-century Christian writer Justin Martyr, who taught in Rome (*Trypho* 38; Rajak 1999), and it has been linked with Jewish references to a prayer against *minim*, an all-purpose word for opponents of Judaism (Janowitz 1998). But we cannot conclude that by Justin's time there was general hostility between Jews and Christians (see below). We do not know how many synagogues there were in the second century, how they were distributed, what their liturgy was, whether it included the prayer against *minim*, and whether these *minim* were Christians.

Given the difficulty of finding contexts for rabbinic discussion, the New Testament is a major source for Judaism in the first-century Mediterranean world, and sometimes it is the only source for a specific practice: for instance, reading and expounding Scripture in weekly meetings at synagogues (ch. 5). Two further first-century sources are Jewish authors who tried to explain Jewish history and teaching to a Roman audience. Philo of Alexandria, writing in the thirties and forties, presented Jewish teaching for an audience that was more familiar with Greek philosophy, and often suggested an allegorical interpretation (ch. 5); his work had much more influence on Christian than on Jewish exegesis. The historian Josephus (Rajak 2003), writing after the destruction of the Temple, tried to explain Judaism in terms of philosophies in the plural, that is, schools of thought that implied a lifestyle. He identified three principal schools: the first two, Pharisees and Sadducees, appear in the New Testament, and the third, Essenes, are probably equivalent to the ascetic, possibly single-sex, community attested in the 'Dead Sea Scrolls' that were found at Qumran just after the Second World War (Campbell 2002).

The Pharisees are a good example of how changes in scholarship have affected interpretation (ch. 1). They are negatively presented in the New Testament, where Jesus is shown challenging legalistic versions of Judaism and declaring that scribes (experts in Jewish law) and Pharisees had allowed rules to obstruct the basic principles of love for God and neighbour: 'woe to you, scribes and Pharisees, hypocrites!' (Matthew 23.23). The letters of Paul (originally Saul) of Tarsus reinforce this perception. Paul, a Pharisee and a vigorous opponent of Christianity, experienced a dramatic conversion while he was travelling from Jerusalem to Damascus (Acts 9.3, hence the phrase 'a Damascus road experience'). Thereafter, he contrasted Jewish adherence to the law with Christian recognition of God's grace (Latin *gratia*, 'favour'), that is, God's free gift to human beings. One of the most far-reaching changes in recent scholarship is widespread recognition that these challenges to Judaism came from Jews. They were 'business as usual' for debates within Judaism (Fredriksen 2002:16), and they do not demonstrate a general distinction between Jews, characterised as rule-governed, exclusive, and unable to recognise God's gift of the Messiah, and Christians, characterised as socially inclusive and active in mission.

Paul made several long journeys to spread the new teaching, and such missionary activity was once thought to be distinctively Christian, on the assumption that Jews did not engage in mission or encourage converts. Converts to Judaism were called 'proselytes', a Greek word for a stranger who comes to live in a new place. Roman law protected Jewish customs, but penalised attempts to impose them on non-Jews; for example, the second-century emperor Antoninus Pius ruled (*Digesta* 48.8.11) that Jews might circumcise their own sons, but a Jew who circumcised anyone else, including his slave, was liable to the penalty for inflicting castration. Once again, interpretation of Jewish practice has changed. There is some evidence for converts, but more for 'godfearers' who did not formally convert, but whose interest in Judaism was encouraged (J. Lieu 2002: 31–68). Jewish practice varied, both in seeking conversion rather than encouraging interest, and in requiring converts to observe Jewish law, including male circumcision (Cohen 1993, Goodman 1994). According to the New Testament (Acts 15), Paul and his fellow-apostle Peter disagreed on whether converts to Christianity should be required to follow Jewish rules on circumcision and on permissible foods, and Peter conceded that Gentiles need not do so. But even in the fourth century, despite vigorous Christian polemic against Judaism, there were still groups that considered themselves to be Christian but followed some Jewish traditions (Mitchell 1999).

Since the later twentieth century, the relationship between Judaism and Christianity has most often been described with images of siblings (Boyarin 1999: 1–9), or as 'the ways that never parted' (Becker and Reed 2003). The formation of distinctive Jewish and Christian orthodoxy has been downdated from the first to the fourth century CE (ch. 6). Early Christianity, on this account, was just another way of being Jewish (Fredriksen and Reinhartz 2002). That leaves unanswered questions whether Christian groups offered something that other varieties of Judaism did not, and in particular whether they were more welcoming to Gentile 'godfearers', or more active in outreach. In the early second century, the Roman philosopher Epictetus used Judaism as an example of making a religious commitment:

Why call yourself a Stoic, why deceive people, why act the part of a Jew when you're Greek? Can't you see why someone is called Jewish or Syrian or Egyptian?

When we see someone in two minds, we say, 'He's not a Jew, he's acting.' But when he takes on the condition of someone who has been baptised and has made the choice, then he really is a Jew and is called a Jew. We too are 'pseudo-baptists', Jews in name but something else in fact, not consistent with rationality, a long way from making use of the principles we are proud to think we know. (Epictetus, *Discourses* 2.9.20–1; Long 2002: 110–1)

This is an interesting example, because baptism was both the Christian initiation rite and a Jewish rite of purification. Epictetus may not have been aware of any difference; and in lecturing to the sons of elite Romans, he did not suggest any difficulty, other than making the commitment, in 'choosing to be a Jew'. To people interested in philosophy, Judaism and Christianity could be understood as philosophical schools offering authoritative texts and an appropriate way of life (Wilken 2003: 73–83).

ON THE MARGINS?

Did Christianity have a special appeal for the poor and the marginal in Roman society?

Go and tell John what you have seen and heard. The blind see again, the lame walk, lepers are cleansed, the deaf hear, the dead are raised, and the poor are given the good news. (Luke 7.22–3)

The Gospels show Jesus teaching among the poor; several of the apostles, including Peter, were fishermen; Paul earned a living by tentmaking, and his letters show that the earliest churches included some people who were far from rich (Meeks 1983). The second-century philosopher Celsus said that Christianity spread among people who lacked education and had only the most basic skills (Origen, *C. Cels.* 3.55, see ch. 5 below). That was inevitable, Origen replied, when so many more people were illiterate than educated. But it is difficult to determine the social level, or the numbers, of Christians, when all we have (as so often in ancient history) is anecdotal evidence from sources who have their own agenda. Early in the second century, Pliny told Trajan (*Epistulae* 10.96) that there were Christians of all ages and ranks in Bithynia, both in towns and in the country. At the end of the century, the Christian writer Tertullian, who came from Carthage, said that there were Christians everywhere, including the imperial palace and the senate (*Apologeticus* 37.4). It would take only one eccentric senator to make that true, for the Christians in the imperial palace might belong to its immense staff of slaves, ranging from servants to civil servants. But by the mid-third century, the emperor Valerian's repression of Christians included

penalties for senators and equestrians (the social rank below senators) and
for leading officials (Cyprian, *Epistulae* 80.2, 258 CE).

Christians could have experienced the rapid growth of their movement
even though the total numbers were very small, and even though some
people who were counted as converts had only a tenuous connection with
the Christian group (Stark 1996; Hopkins 1998). Comparisons across time
and culture are always risky, but it may be helpful to consider protest
marches: the organisers and the police estimate numbers differently, people
join the march for many reasons, and far more join the march than continue
to be involved with the cause. Material culture does not help with the
problem of numbers. Until the third century, Christians met in houses or
in hired rooms that cannot easily be identified as churches (White 1990),
especially as decoration and imagery used the common tradition that was
shared with non-Christians (Elsner 1998, 2003). Some Christians may have
continued to attend Jewish synagogues or other meeting-places, but these
too are difficult to identify; and even when Christian or Jewish meeting-
places can be identified, it is difficult or impossible to tell how many people
they served, especially in country districts (G. Clark 2001b; Schwartz 2001:
216–39).

Another suggestion about the spread of Christianity is that it appealed
especially to people who wanted more recognition of their ability or their
wealth than Roman society allowed, and experienced 'status dissonance'
(Meeks 1983). There were opportunities for such people in many varieties
of religion. Thus prosperous ex-slaves, or resident foreigners, who were
unlikely to achieve priesthood in a traditional cult, might hold office in
elective cults or as *Augustales* with responsibility for local cult (Beard–
North–Price 1998: 1.358). Christian local leadership at first used the strengths
and resources of individuals, and Paul's letters show that some groups had a
'supervisor' (*episkopos*), some a group of elders (*presbuteroi*); both forms of
church government (episcopalian and presbyterian) continue to this day.
By the early second century, a hierarchy had developed, and there was a
widespread structure of bishop (*episkopos*), who might supervise more than
one church in a region; priest (*presbuteros* again) who was the bishop's
deputy in charge of a church; and deacon (*diakonos*, literally 'servant' or
'administrator'; Latin *minister*).

Women were not part of this hierarchy, nor did they leave authoritative
Christian writings: there are no Mothers of the Church, and 'matristics'
(by analogy with 'patristics', ch. 1) rests on a handful of texts and sayings
that are ascribed to women. This is not surprising in the context of Roman
society, where women had civic rights but did not hold public office or

elect those who did, and were thought to be unsuited to roles of public responsibility (G. Clark 1993). Early Christian texts name women as supporters and benefactors of churches, just as Jewish inscriptions honour them as supporters and benefactors of synagogues (Brooten 1982), and the cities of the Roman empire honour them and give them statues and titles as benefactors of cities (Van Bremen 1996). None of these women can be shown to have held office, chaired a meeting, or led a congregation; in Christian tradition, the declaration 'I do not permit a woman to teach' (1 Timothy 2.12) was ascribed to the authoritative Paul. Women lacked formal education, and were thought to be especially susceptible to false teaching (J. Lieu 2002: 83–99), so one way of attacking rival groups was to say that women were too influential within them (Beard–North–Price 1998: 1.299–300). But even without such hostility, modest and well-behaved women were expected to resist any public role.[5]

The status of women is one of the most interesting examples of Roman culture surviving in church tradition (ch. 1). In the 1970s and 1980s, there was intense debate in the Church of England on whether women can be ordained (from Latin *ordinare*, to 'appoint to office') as priests. Opponents argued that early church practice is normative, because Jesus chose the apostles who established it. A few also argued that women are weak, or seductive, or not suited to leadership roles, or essentially domestic, just as traditional Romans said. Supporters attempted to show that early church practice included women who were in effect ordained, but that their status had been misrepresented or ignored by a tradition hostile to women (Fiorenza 1983). They also argued that early Christianity offered women greater affirmation than other religious options could provide. Jesus taught and healed women; in a culture that did not accept their testimony in law, women were the earliest witnesses of his resurrection; Paul declared that 'there is neither Jew nor Greek, slave nor free, male nor female, for you are all one in Christ Jesus' (Galatians 3.28). But Paul was talking about spiritual equality, and he was not alone in affirming the spiritual equality of women and simultaneously maintaining their traditional social roles: these were standard assumptions of Platonist and Stoic philosophy (G. Clark 1993: 120–1). Slaves, likewise, were told that they were spiritually no different from free people, but they could not expect their church to buy them out

---

[5] Cameron 1996, updating her 1980 challenge to optimistic interpretations by New Testament scholars, provides a brief history of work on women and Christianity in the intervening years. Kraemer, 1988 and 1992, covers Roman and Jewish as well as Christian evidence. Castelli 1998 (with extensive bibliography), responding to Stark 1996 on the role of women in the spread of Christianity, is a nuanced and detailed survey of status, demography and representation.

or their Christian owner to free them; rather, they were to serve the better for love of Christ (Ephesians 6: 5–8; see further Garnsey 1996). One slave, Callistus, became a bishop in third-century Rome, but he was a special kind of slave, the financial agent of a member of the emperor's household (Hippolytus, *Refutatio Omnium Haeresium* 9.12). Christianity did not offer unusual opportunities for status: what it did offer was moral and religious teaching, and shared ritual, that extended to women, slaves and the poor (ch. 5).

CHRISTIANS AGAINST CHRISTIANS: HERESY

Christian groups were also distinctive in attacking rival theologies, using all the weapons provided by Roman rhetorical training. They denounced traditional Roman religion (see below) and sought to differentiate Christianity from Judaism (see above). In particular, whereas Judaism in the early centuries CE expected disagreements that could not be resolved (Boyarin 1999), Christians tried to eliminate rival interpretations of Christianity. Pagans, Jews and heretics were the 'others' against whom the vocal majority defined itself and its beliefs. Until recently, minority interpretations of Christian belief and practice were known (like anti-Christian arguments, above) only from refutations by the winning side, which called them heresies. 'Heresy' comes from *hairesis*, literally 'choice' or 'option', the standard Greek word for a school of thought in medicine or philosophy. Philosophers and doctors of course challenged each other's choices, and contrasted wrong choices with thinking aright, but Christians were especially vehement in distinguishing orthodoxy (Greek *orthodoxia*, 'right-thinking') from heresy. Some scholars think that this Christian characteristic created a culture of intolerance in the formerly tolerant Roman society (Athanassiadi 2002). Others think that in the early centuries CE there was a general preoccupation with the correct interpretation of texts (ch. 5), and that Jewish debates about the law, or philosophic debates about what Plato meant, are independent of Christian influence, or (Boys-Stones 2001) themselves influenced Christian debates about orthodoxy.

Christians had strong motives for concern about correct belief. Just as doctors might have said, of another medical *hairesis*, 'these people kill their patients', heresy was a question of everlasting life or everlasting death. In the late fourth century, John Chrysostom said of one wrong belief, namely that Christians were required to observe Jewish law, that it was as if a condemned criminal refused a free pardon from the emperor (*Adversus Iudaeos* 2.1.6). People who were identified as heretics were 'excommunicated': that is, they were excluded from the Christian community and from the rituals that expressed community, especially from the sharing of bread and wine in the eucharist, which is often called 'holy communion'. But it was quite possible for individuals or groups to be in communion with some churches and excommunicated by others. Disagreements were all the stronger because charges of heresy were often accompanied by further charges of immoral or criminal behaviour (another well-known rhetorical technique), even in the centuries before heretics became liable to legal penalties or, if they were important enough, to exile (ch. 6).

In the mid-second century, Irenaeus of Lyon wrote a long treatise *Against Heresies*. According to his model, heretics culpably diverge from orthodoxy, usually through intellectual arrogance or moral corruption, and the resultant struggle tests and strengthens the church's faith. Early Christian writers accepted this model (R.Williams 1989), and were confident that from the beginnings of Christianity the catholic (Greek *katholikos*, 'universal') church had held orthodox (Greek *orthodoxos*, 'right-thinking') beliefs, and that these beliefs could be clearly distinguished from the false beliefs called heresy.[6] Twentieth-century scholarship challenged the model, arguing that orthodoxy emerged from the debate with heresy (this is often called the 'Bauer hypothesis', in tribute to Bauer 1972); and new discoveries of texts made it possible to reinterpret 'heretical' teachings.

Second-century Gnosticism is one example of reinterpretation (Behr 2000: 17–21; K. King 2003). According to Irenaeus, who cited some of their texts, Gnostics claimed that they had special knowledge (Greek *gnōsis*) revealed only to a spiritual elite. Other Christians accused them of extreme sexual licence (ch. 1): this is one possible consequence of contempt for the body, for why should sexual licence matter if the body does not? They were also said to be female-dominated (see above). But when some of the texts were rediscovered, at Nag Hammadi in Egypt, it became much easier to understand how intelligent people might have believed what Irenaeus presented as dangerous nonsense. 'Gnostic' is now a questionable category (M. Williams 1996) because it is too general to be useful, and 'gnostic' texts can be interpreted as elaborate mythic retellings of the relationship between God and the world, closely connected with philosophical debates about different levels of being. They have even been printed in the form of a traditional Bible (Layton 1987) to make the point that this was one among many versions of Christianity, and they have attracted interest from

---

[6] This is not the distinction between (Roman) Catholic and Protestant churches, or between (Eastern) Orthodox and western churches. They belong to a later stage of church controversy.

some feminist theologians because of the role they give to female divine powers.

Another example of reinterpretation is the teaching of Mani, which spread westward and eastward from third-century Mesopotamia. 'Manichaean' is still used to mean a stark opposition of good and evil, and an extreme hostility to the body. Manichaeism was illegal in the later Roman empire, because it came from enemy territory east of the river Euphrates, and because its followers formed secret cells, sometimes within Christian churches. Manichaean books were publicly burned (ch. 3). So the main evidence for Manichaean teachings came from Augustine, who as a young man spent nine years as a Manichaean 'hearer', then, in the late fourth century, vehemently rejected the teachings. But in the later twentieth century some Manichaean texts were rediscovered, including psalm-texts in Coptic,[7] and the 'Mani codex', a miniature anthology on the life of Mani, in Greek translation from Aramaic. Manichaeism was a religion of beautiful and authoritative books (ch. 5), and it too offered an elaborate mythological system that can be connected with philosophy.[8]

Why, then, were these teachings, and those who advanced them, so furiously attacked? It was not just a struggle for power within the Christian churches: debates with 'heresy' brought fundamental beliefs into focus. Gnostics were understood to teach, as many philosophers did, that the material world is the lowest level of being, and the human body is an obstruction to the soul. Manichaeans were understood to teach a dualist system in which the power of Light is opposed by a power of Darkness that has caused the material world, and the human body and its desires are alien to the immortal soul. But Judaeo-Christian scripture teaches that the world, and the human body, is God's creation, flawed by human sin but essentially good. If the body is only a distraction for the soul, and perhaps was made by an evil power, how could it be argued that Jesus Christ, who lived as an embodied human being, reconciled God and humanity?

This is the central Christian doctrine of incarnation (Latin *caro* means 'flesh', and by extension 'body'), sometimes expressed as 'Jesus is God in human form' (see further Ward 2000: 44–55). It was very difficult for Romans to accept that a divine being could also be a human being who

---

[7] Coptic is Egyptian written in Greek letters with some extra signs and many Greek loan-words. It apparently began in the late first century CE. Smith 1998 surveys late-antique Coptic literature, and J. Robinson 1988 translates the Nag Hammadi texts.

[8] Valantasis 2000 includes translations of Manichaean texts, with some discussion; a fuller range in Lieu and Gardner 2003; BeDuhn 2000 for sympathetic interpretation.

suffered death on the cross. There was revulsion at the thought of the divine contaminated by messy, decaying mortality, for divine beings were by definition immortal; they were also invulnerable, since anything that affected them would have to be stronger than they were. One solution was to say that Christ only seemed to be a human being who died, but was really a divine being in disguise, like Roman gods who might make an appearance on earth. (Thus in upland Asia Minor, local people identified the eloquent Paul and his imposing colleague Barnabas as Hermes and Zeus, Acts 14.11–13.) This solution is traditionally called the 'docetist' heresy, from Greek *dokei*, 's/he seems'. It has several variants: the executioners were deceived by the superior power of Christ; or Simon of Cyrene, who carried his cross, was crucified in his place; or Jesus did not actually die on the cross, but revived from coma after he was taken down. (In one bizarrely popular modern variation, he not only revived, but also married Mary of Magdala and raised a family in Marseilles; but modern versions of the theory are advanced to explain why his followers thought he had overcome death, not to explain that he did not experience death.) But if Jesus did not, and could not, really die on the cross, he could not really share the human experience of death and dereliction, and there remains an unbridgeable gap between God and humanity. So the 'docetist heresy' prompted further reflection on the relationship of Jesus Christ to God and to humanity.

That reflection continued in the great theological debates of the fourth and fifth centuries, which were also presented as a struggle to defend orthodoxy from the onslaughts of heresy. Arius, an early fourth-century theologian from Alexandria, and Athanasius, who became bishop of Alexandria, differed on the fundamental question of incarnation: how could Jesus Christ be understood as fully human and as fully divine, so that he reconciled humanity with God? Arius, whose views survive almost entirely through the counter-arguments of his opponents, seems to have argued that Scripture required a distinction between Christ and all other created beings, but also between Christ and God the Father. As late as the early twentieth century Arius was under attack as the archetypal heretic, who relied too much on philosophy and too little on faith, denied the full divinity of Christ, and thereby rejected the reconciliation offered by God. His theology, it was said, was decisively rejected at the first ecumenical[9] church

---

[9] An 'ecumenical' council is literally a world council (Greek *oikoumenē*, 'the inhabited world'). In practice, it was usually like a present-day 'international' conference: that is, it brought together delegates from the region where it was held, and a few from further afield.

council, held at Nicaea in 325 and presided over by the emperor Constantine (ch. 6). But by the 1960s it seemed clear that fourth-century debate had been over-simplified and misunderstood, and that present-day Christians had something to learn from Arius (R. Williams 2001).

The statement of belief agreed at Nicaea (not identical with the statement now known as the Nicene creed) affirmed that Christ is 'of the same substance' (Greek *homoousios*) as God the Father. The Greek prefix *homo*- means 'same', and *ousia* means 'essential being': thus the disciples Peter and John, who are two people, are 'of the same substance' in that both are human beings. But, as Arius pointed out, *homoousios* is not Biblical language; and as many historians and theologians have pointed out, the 'agreed statement' from a large-scale meeting is very different from serious reflection on theology. The council of Nicaea did not end this debate. Some fourth-century theologians argued that Christ should be called simply 'like' the Father (Greek *homoios*, hence 'homoean' theology), others that he should be acknowledged as 'unlike' (Greek *anomoios*). How could Christ be 'like' God, or of the same essential being, if he shared the human experiences of limited knowledge and power? But how could he be human if he did not experience human limitations and desires? Did he have both a divine and a human nature, and if so, how were they related? The council of Chalcedon (451) produced an influential response to these questions. It rejected the 'monophysite' account of Christ as having only one, divine, nature, and insisted that Christ was both fully human and fully divine. Chalcedon led to long-lasting divisions, made worse because language barriers caused misunderstanding between Latin- and Greek-speaking churches (Hanson 1989; Brown 2002: 100–11 for the social and political context). Here too there has been revaluation, and theologians avoid the term 'monophysite' as a misrepresentation (they prefer 'miaphysite', 'having one [united] nature').

This discussion of Christians and others started from the problem of sources for what non-Christians thought about Christians. It has tried to show how some of the probable reasons for Christian success were also reasons for traditional Romans to think of Christians as anti-social and subversive. It has asked what Christianity offered that other religious options did not, and in doing so, it has questioned the sharp distinction between Christians and Jews that is made in early Christian texts. It has shown how quite recent discoveries have led to reinterpretation of teachings that had been classed as heresy. Christians and Jews, orthodox and heretic, are contrasts that need to be softened or complicated. One traditional contrast remains: pagans and Christians.

PAGANS

The word 'pagan' is widely, but reluctantly, used by historians: reluctantly because it was Christian disparagement of non-Christians, widely because it is difficult to find an alternative. *Paganus* may have meant 'hick', because a *pagus* was a little village (compare 'heathen', from German *heiden*, 'heath'). Or, if *paganus* was army slang for 'civilian', it meant someone who had not enlisted in the service of Christ. 'I am a Christian' was a chosen identity, but the people Christians called 'pagans' did not have a word for themselves. If the question arose, as it did in the mid-third century (ch. 3), they need only say 'I have always worshipped the gods.' But after Constantine gave official support to Christianity, followers of the traditional religion did need a name, and their problem demonstrates the diversity of Roman religion. In the mid-fourth century the emperor Julian reclaimed the term Hellene ('Greek') for followers of the traditional religion, on the grounds that true religion was bound up with Greek culture and philosophy (ch. 5). But his Christian subjects objected that they were Greeks too, and as his reign was very short (eighteen months, 361–3), it is not known whether the Latin-speaking half of his empire would have accepted 'Hellene'. In the early fifth century, a philosophically educated correspondent of Augustine called himself *paganus* (*Ep.* 234.1): this may be deliberate acceptance of a disparaging name that had entered Roman law (ch. 6).

Some modern writers use 'polytheist', but though there is a Greek adjective *polutheos* ('of many gods'), neither Greek nor Latin provided a word for someone who believes that there are many gods. Moreover, many philosophically trained Greeks and Romans were not, strictly speaking, polytheist, for they believed that the many gods of traditional cult were subordinates of the one god or manifestations of the single divine power. This position is sometimes called 'henotheist', a modern term for belief in one supreme god, as distinct from monotheist belief in only one god; it is also called 'soft monotheism', belief in one god that allows for lesser divine beings (Fowden 1998; Athanassiadi and Frede 1999, reviewed by T. Barnes 2001). It is comparable to versions of Jewish monotheism that give very high status to Moses or to the Messiah or to angels; or to some accounts of the relationship of Jesus Christ to God, especially when those accounts are combined with popular devotion to saints and angels (for cults of angels, see Peers 2001: 6–9). Much recent scholarship argues that this 'soft monotheism' was widespread in the Roman world of the early centuries CE, so one reason for the success of Christianity was that the ground was already prepared (Liebeschuetz 2000).

   Christian polemic presented traditional Roman religion as worshipping
a multitude of idols (ch. 1). These man-made images, Christians argued,
were obviously powerless: how can you reverence a god when you know
the man who made it? Or if the images did have some power, that was
because demons had taken up residence in them, and had deluded people into offering them sacrifice. 'Demons' are *daimones*, the traditional
Greek word for lesser divine beings: in philosophical texts they may be
benign powers, but in Christian texts they are malevolent. 'The gods of
the nations are demons' (Psalms 96.4) was a favourite Bible quotation. So
Christian writers said that it was hardly surprising if Roman society had
deplorably low moral standards, its culture encouraged extravagant display,
and its laws allowed men to commit adultery and to reject their newborn
children (ch. 6). This was only to be expected, because, under demonic
influence, the traditional religion failed to offer any moral teaching, and its
festivals presented stories about gods behaving badly. But these Christian
attacks borrowed extensively from Roman philosophical critique of religious practices, and from the bitter social commentary deployed in Roman
satire. (The critique has remarkable powers of survival. 'Pagan' is still widely
associated with uninhibited sexuality, and 'Roman' with 'orgy', which is
a hostile interpretation of Greek *orgia*, one form of religious ritual.) Thus
the Christian Lactantius and the anti-Christian Porphyry, in the late third
century, have a common stock of examples and of rhetoric denouncing
empty images, delusive demons, and the allegedly wise who mislead the
simple (Digeser 2000).
   Philosophy is the great exception to the general predominance of
mainstream Christian sources. A wide range of Greek and Roman philosophical writing survives, and it includes moral exhortation; records of
self-examination and spiritual experience; critique of traditional religious
practice, especially of animal sacrifice; and philosophical theology. In the
early centuries CE, the most influential philosophy was Platonism. Plato
taught that there is a single divine power, and that God is necessarily good:
to say that God does harm is like saying that heat makes things cold. A
being that was not good would not be worthy of worship. People must aim
to become like God, and this means that they must use their God-given
reason to strengthen their immortal soul: they must work to understand
what goodness is, and must regulate their desires by reason so that they
live rightly (ch. 4). There remains a question (J. Barnes 2002) how far
philosophy reached beyond the social elite who could afford an education.
Augustine commented in the early fifth century that Romans said that

philosophy taught morality, but there were no temples to Plato (*City of God (De Civitate Dei)* 2.7: see further ch. 5).

But the more we understand about religious options in the early centuries CE (J. Smith 1990), the more difficult it is to answer the great historical question. Why did Christianity survive and succeed in Roman society? It was easier to explain when most scholars accepted the early Christian claims that Judaism, though ethically and religiously superior to Roman religion, was rule-bound and exclusive, and that Roman religion was a system of traditional cults without ethical or spiritual content. But if many Jewish communities welcomed the adherents they called 'godfearers', and were also open to less committed gentile sympathisers, Romans who had unfulfilled spiritual needs could opt for this ancient monotheist tradition with its strong social ethic. Alternatively, Romans who had a philosophical education could see traditional Roman cults as appropriate for simple people, perhaps conveying hidden truths through myth and ritual, and acceptable because the gods they honoured were manifestations of the one god. Why would they choose the one religious option that could get them executed for subversion? The next chapter considers the Christian claim that martyrdom actually made converts: as Tertullian put it (*Apol.* 50.13), 'the blood of Christians is seed'.

CHAPTER 3

The blood of the martyrs

The people's flag is deepest red:
It's shrouded oft our martyred dead.
And ere their bones grow stiff and cold
Their hearts' blood dyed its every fold.
So raise the scarlet standard high,
Beneath its shade we'll live or die.
(James O'Connell, 'The Red Flag', 1899)

Your cruelties, each more refined than the last, achieve nothing. They attract others to our school. Each time you mow us down, you increase our number: the blood of Christians is seed. Many of you preach endurance of pain and death: Cicero in the *Tusculans*, Seneca in *Chance*, Diogenes, Pyrrho, Callinicus. But their words do not find as many followers as the Christians do in teaching by actions.
(Tertullian, *Apol.* 50.13–14, 197 CE)

Jesus died on a cross: a public, agonising death, legally inflicted by a Roman provincial governor as the standard punishment for rebels. For almost three hundred years, his followers were also at risk of legally inflicted death, sometimes as a public spectacle. Roman law allowed Christians to be burned alive or thrown to wild animals or inventively tortured. But after two millennia of Christian imagery, people do not connect Roman legal penalties with Amnesty reports. Some people wear a crucifix, a model of a man fastened to a cross (Latin *cruci fixus*), as an item of jewellery. 'Christians 0, lions 43, in sudden-death overtime' does not provoke the same response as a news report of a zoo-keeper mauled to death, or of a prisoner on Death Row.

Traditional Christian accounts of martyrdom must bear some of the blame for this indifference. They deal in standardised marvels. Hagiography (Greek *hagios*, 'holy'), writing about saints, nowadays means 'uncritically reverent biography' or even 'pious fiction'. There is evidence from many contexts that religious commitment helps people to withstand torture, and that people suffering immediate shock may not experience pain: but

38

hagiographic narratives describe feats of physical endurance and serenity that are very hard to believe (Delehaye 1905; Heffernan 1988).[1] In these stories, victims confidently defy the torturers, burning flesh smells as sweet as baking bread, repeated assaults fail to kill martyrs, corpses resist decay and dispersal. Visual representations of martyrdom also sanitise the death and emphasise the serene confidence of the martyr, to such an extent that the soldier-martyr St Sebastian, shot full of arrows, has become a gay icon (Wyke 1998). Everyday English trivialises the language of torture: 'we all have our crosses to bear', 'don't make a martyr out of him', 'she's a martyr to indigestion'. But Roman repression of Christianity must be taken seriously, both out of respect for human suffering, and because martyrdom was so important for the self-understanding of Christians both before and after the danger ended.

WHY MAKE MARTYRS?

Why did Romans make martyrs of Christians? *Martures* is Greek for 'witnesses': a martyr bears witness to his or her principles by choosing to suffer or die rather than renounce them. Christian use of the name 'martyr' was new, and Christians had a distinctive confidence in reward after death (Bowersock 1995: 5–16), but they were not the only people to die for their beliefs. According to Plato, the Athenians executed Socrates because he would not abandon a divine commission to seek wisdom. There was a tradition of Greek and Roman philosophers who defied torture and execution by tyrants, and there were Jewish heroes, most famously the Maccabees, who endured torture and death rather than assimilate to the religion of the ruling power. All these helped to shape Christian accounts of martyrs confronting their judges and facing death (Rajak 1997, Alexander 2002). But Christians were martyred as a public spectacle in a Roman amphitheatre, a form of death that declared them to be outcasts from Roman society. They first appear in Roman non-Christian texts as the victims of legal violence, hideously executed on the orders of the emperor Nero as scapegoats for the fire that destroyed much of central Rome in 64 (ch. 2).

Christians were executed because their refusal to worship the Roman gods entailed refusal to obey the Roman authorities, and because they aroused suspicions of anti-social behaviour (ch. 2). Our sources for these executions are almost without exception Christian. For Christians, the martyrdom

---

[1] The *Acta Sanctorum* ('Acts of the Saints') have been edited since the seventeenth century by the Bollandists (named after John van Bolland) of the Jesuit order, who publish *Analecta Bollandiana*. Musurillo 1972 provides text and translation of some famous early martyr-acts; a revision is in progress.

of Christians was of very great importance: it was recorded in detail and commemorated on the anniversary of the death, and any relics of martyrs were preserved and revered (see below). Non-Christians hardly mention it. When Pliny wrote to Trajan about his interrogation and execution of Christians (ch. 2), his main concern was to get official validation. He followed standard procedure in the use of torture to get legally valid testimony from two slave women, but his letter does not mention any other use of legal violence on the accused, or suggest that those he executed died with any extreme penalty. Trajan's successor Hadrian confirmed Trajan's policy in response to the proconsul of Asia Minor (Eus. *EH* 4.9): charges against Christians must be made in the proper form, not by public outcry; anyone who makes a false accusation should be punished; the proconsul should decide the penalty if it can be proved that the accused has done anything contrary to the laws.

An official imperial response (rescript) had legal force, and Christians used Hadrian's rescript to argue that being a Christian was not in itself a ground for conviction. The source for this rescript is Christian: Eusebius (ch. 1) says that Justin (mid-second century) reported it, and that he has translated it from the Latin original. It is also a Christian source, Lactantius (*Divinae Institutiones* 5.11.9, early fourth century), who reports that the great jurist Ulpian (early third century) included in his handbook for regional governors the imperial rescripts that related to charges against Christians. Similarly, only Christian authors comment on the penalties imposed by Roman governors. According to Tertullian (*Ad Scapulam* 4.3), one governor of Africa (present-day north Africa) told Christians how to answer so that he could dismiss the case. A governor of Asia Minor (*Scap.* 5.1) executed some Christians who reported themselves to him, but told the rest that if they really wanted to die, there were plenty of ropes and cliffs at their disposal. There is no evidence for what those governors thought about religion, or about the immediate political situation, but in one famous case there may be some indication of the governor's view. The story of Perpetua (see below), martyred in Carthage in 203, names the governor who condemned her as Hilarianus. If this is the same Hilarianus who set up an inscription in Spain, its unusual wording suggests that he had strong views on which gods should or should not be worshipped (Rives 1996), and may therefore have been especially hostile to Christians.

Tertullian observed (*Apol.* 10) that other people are tortured to make them confess; only Christians are tortured to make them deny. From the Christian perspective, a Christian on trial 'confessed' Christ in the sense that he or she acknowledged (Latin *confessus/a est*) faith in Christ. But from the other point of view, to acknowledge oneself a Christian was to confess at least disloyalty and recalcitrance, and at worst defiance of the gods and criminal conspiracy against the social order (ch. 2). Christian writers insisted, correctly, that no law actually required a Roman judge to condemn Christians just for being Christians (T. Barnes 1968). But Roman governors could decide whether and how to 'take notice' (*cognitio*) of a case, that is, to deal with it in their capacity as judges. They could condemn Christians for 'the name' alone, and they had the 'right of the sword', *ius gladii*, that authorised them to impose the death penalty. Pliny (ch. 2) correctly referred Roman citizens to the emperor, but after 212 all free inhabitants of the Roman empire were formally citizens, and appeal was less likely. The form of the death penalty varied with social status. From the second century, if not earlier, the free poor were liable to physical punishment that had once been reserved for slaves (Garnsey 1970), so for the lower orders (*humiliores*), death could come with 'extreme penalties', as a public spectacle in the arena. For the 'more respectable' (*honestiores*), it would usually mean beheading; but in some circumstances, especially where treason was suspected, rank was no protection.

SPECTATOR SPORT?

Just as Christian martyrdom was shaped by Roman penal codes, so Christian accounts of martyrdom were shaped by the official record, the 'things done' (Latin *acta*) of a Roman trial; indeed, martyr-narratives are a major source for court procedure (B. Shaw 2003: 553). The story of a martyrdom is often called the *acta* of the martyr; alternatively, it is called the *passio* (plural *passiones*), 'suffering', of the martyr. The narrative focuses on interrogation and perhaps torture, sentencing, custody and death (Barnes 1985: 143–86 surveys variations in practice and narrative). The official record of a trial had to show that the accused had been asked the proper questions, warned of the consequences, given time for reflection, and sentenced in accordance with the law (Harries 1999a: 110). The first question, a request for name and social status, determined the procedure that was followed and the penalties that could be imposed. These were different for slave and free, Roman citizens and non-citizens, but not for men and women (except in that pregnancy deferred execution: C. Jones 1993). Martyr-acts sometimes report that a Christian asked for name and status replied 'I am a Christian', for that was the only identity that mattered. In the late fourth century, Jerome described a dream in which he was dragged before the judge (*Epistulae* 22). He said 'I am a Christian', but the judge replied 'You lie: you are a Ciceronian' (ch. 5), and he was flogged until the bystanders pleaded for mercy on his youth.

This dream, like many others (B. Shaw 2003) reported during and after the centuries of persecution, reflects Christian accounts of interrogation. In these accounts, some of the reported dialogue between judge and accused could plausibly come from a court record, but some of the fuller description could not. A pioneering study of martyr-narratives (Delehaye 1905) suggested that the simpler accounts are earlier and more likely to be authentic; but simplicity can itself be a rhetorical technique, and a simple narrative style may require a skilled narrator (ch. 5). In the more elaborate accounts, the stereotypical 'angry judge' (Harries 1999b) tries in vain to make the Christian renounce his or her faith. The judge alternates threats of torture and death with appeals to concern for family, but the Christian confidently proclaims his or her faith, and the judge, who should be able to control himself and others, is overcome by rage and frustration. Where a court record would simply note the instruction to use torture, Christian accounts describe in detail what was done to the martyr, whose serene endurance enrages the torturers and exhausts their strength. A court record would note the sentence of death, but in Christian accounts the sentence is a victory for the martyr and a defeat for the judge, and the execution is also described in detail. The *Passio Perpetuae*, which narrates the martyrdom of Perpetua at Carthage in 203, is an especially striking example.

The *Passio Perpetuae* has been intensively studied (B. Shaw 1993, P. Miller 1994, Salisbury 1998) because most of it is presented as Perpetua's own record, written in prison. This is doubly remarkable, both because it is a martyr's story and because it is a woman's. Almost no writings by women survive from the ancient world, and when they do, someone is sure to argue that they were really written by a man. Perpetua, according to her *passio*, was a young woman of Carthage, well educated and from a respectable family; at the time of her arrest she had a baby son. Her husband does not appear in the story; her father tries to persuade her to renounce her faith and is beaten, on the governor's orders, for his persistence. In her dreams, she has greater spiritual power than the hierarchy of her church; finally, she dreams that she becomes physically a man to fight her opponent in the arena (see below, ch. 4, for heroic women reclassified as men). Another writer takes over to report her death. She and her slave Felicitas, who had recently given birth, were stripped and sent out to confront a wild cow. The crowd protested, not at their being killed, but at their nakedness, and they were called back to be clothed. Then they were sent out again. Perpetua eventually had to be killed by a nervous gladiator, who bungled his first attempt.

Martyrs were displayed to the Roman public as naked and tortured bodies, and martyr-acts display them again. Why do Christian texts insist on the detail of pain and insult, and what are we to think about the people who wrote and heard and read them? From a Roman perspective, execution with extreme penalties was meant to be degrading. The community that eagerly watched the death expressed its rejection of the criminal. The audience in an amphitheatre was a microcosm of society, ranked in accordance with social order, the best seats going to social and religious leaders. The victims in the arena with the wild beasts were social outcasts, rebels or criminals convicted of atrocities. Even now, many people react to the murder or abuse of children, or to terrorist attacks, by demanding that the guilty should be seen to suffer: 'hanging's too good for them'.

Christian writers claimed that the crowds who watched Christian deaths were awed by the serene courage of the martyrs, and that some were inspired to convert. Tertullian's famous phrase 'the blood of Christians is seed' (*Apol.* 50.13, quoted above) has a special significance. 'Seed' translates *semen*, and according to Roman medical theory, the male seed that begets new life is made of refined blood (below, ch. 4). But the reaction of non-Christians to these public deaths might be quite different. A man covered in blood might be met with a shout of *Salvum lotum*, 'Enjoyed your bath?' (*Passio Perp.* 21), the usual greeting for someone who had just come from the baths. (Christians could reinterpret this mockery as 'washed and saved'.) More thoughtful spectators might react with pity for the deluded, with revulsion from their rejection of family and society, or with puzzled horror at their readiness to die.[2]

Marcus Aurelius, the Roman emperor (mid-second century) who tried to live as a philosopher, included in his *Meditations* a comment on the Christian attitude to death. The soul, he says, must be ready to leave the body, but this readiness must come 'not from sheer obstinacy, like the Christians, but with reason and dignity, and, so as to convince others, without being stagy' (11.3). In 177 Marcus confirmed death-sentences on Roman citizens from Lyon and Vienne, in southern France, who had been

---

[2] At the time of writing, there is a comparable range of reactions to suicide bombers. Some people think they are brainwashed or deluded; some take them as typical of their religion; some call them cowards, presumably because they do not fight openly; some call for vengeance on their families; some try to understand what could make someone choose to commit random murder by suicide. Christian martyrs died but did not kill.

arrested as Christians. It does not follow that he personally authorised the appalling public torture that the local governor, perhaps in response to mob violence, inflicted on non-citizens and on one citizen (Eus. *EH* 5.1.3–63). Galen, court doctor to Marcus, is alone among non-Christian writers in having (apparently) made a partially favourable comment on the Christian attitude to death. This comment survives, not in his voluminous extant works on medicine and philosophy, but in an Arabic quotation from one of his lost works. Elsewhere, he disapproved of Jews and Christians for relying on faith rather than demonstration (ch. 5); but one remark, supposedly from his summary of Plato's *Republic*, praises Christians for their contempt of death and their restraint in sexual matters (Wilken 2003: 79–80).

Contempt for death coexisted with close attention, in early Christian texts, to physical suffering and dead bodies. There are theological reasons for this: physical suffering can be seen as sharing in the suffering of Christ, and Christian belief in resurrection strengthened belief in the continuing power of the holy dead (see below, and ch. 4, on relics). Non-Christian literature, in the early centuries CE, also shows concern for the body in pain or dismembered (Perkins 1995). This general concern may be a cultural response to Christian martyrdom (Bowersock 1994), comparable to the literature of illness prompted by TB in the late nineteenth century and AIDS in the late twentieth. But it is the Christian texts that describe in detail bodies undergoing torture, or showing the physical effects of extreme asceticism (ch. 4). In the last twenty years, the questions asked about these texts have changed. The main question used to be how, if at all, these stereotyped and improbable narratives could be used as historical evidence, especially for the lives of the poor who came to the saint for help (ch. 6); the best hope was the local detail (see for example Lane Fox 1997). Then attention moved to the envisaged audience. It may seem frivolous to call martyr-acts 'gore-nography', or 'body-rippers', but these labels make a point about what seems to be the marketing of violence. Many present-day readers are shocked by the textual display of tortured bodies, especially female bodies, and by the stylisation of torture (Burrus 1995, G. Clark 1998).

A pessimistic reading suggests that these accounts appeal to a corrupt, and still recognisable, taste for eroticised violence: the audience envisaged by martyr-acts would now watch video nasties or, worse, snuff movies in which people actually die. An optimistic reading suggests that the purpose is to show the triumph of the victim over the worst that Roman society can do to him or her. The audience identifies with the martyr, not with the torturer. The martyr's pain is not forgotten: it is commemorated, admired and given meaning, and that meaning is different from the degradation intended by the torturer (Tilley 1996). In the late fourth century, the Latin poet Prudentius wrote a sequence *On the [Martyrs'] Crowns* (known by the Greek title *Peristephanōn*; see further Roberts 1993). Martyrs were symbolically crowned because, like athletes or gladiators, they had won a contest; they are often depicted carrying the palm-branch that was presented to victors. In one of these poems (*Per.* 3), the girl Eulalia – who is ready for marriage, so aged about twelve – counts the marks of the torturer's 'claw' on her side and interprets them as Christ written on her body. In another, an angel records the exact dimensions of every wound on the martyr's body and measures every drop of blood (*Per.* 10.1121–30). The martyr's pain is significant because he or she has a share in the suffering of Christ, and Christian teaching on creation, incarnation and resurrection means that the body is not to be disregarded (see below, and ch. 4).

Another explanation for narratives of martyrdom sets the martyr's contest within the Roman tradition of spectacle (Kyle 1998: 242–64). The Romans are the only people known to have staged, as entertainment, fights that were expected to end in death. Here again, some scholars take an optimistic view, pointing out that gladiator-fights were not just entertainment: they were part of religious festivals, an offering to the gods. Moreover, trained gladiators were an expensive investment, and unless the spectators insisted, their owners preferred them not to die. Some scholars argue further that criminals who were sentenced to fight with humans or wild animals could redeem themselves by facing death with courage, and that watching the fight was itself a training in courage (Wiedemann 1992). But educated Romans who commented on the public shows did not take this line. Instead, they declared their revulsion from the bloodshed, the cruelty of the crowd, and the assumption that the gods wanted such offerings. In the late fourth century, Augustine denounced gladiator fights to his rhetoric students, even before he was a committed Christian. The most convincing account of watching gladiators is the famous passage of his *Confessions* (6.7.11–8.13) on his friend Alypius, who had tried to break his addiction to fights, but was dragged along by friends. At first he shut his eyes, then a great roar from the crowd made him look. A gladiator was down:

As he saw that blood, he drank in savagery, and did not turn away. His gaze was riveted, he absorbed madness, and he did not know it. He was delighted by the competition in crime, he was drunk on bloodthirsty pleasure. He was not now the one who had come, he was one of the crowd to which he had come, and a true associate of those who had brought him. (*Conf.* 6.8.13)

Christian emperors banned gladiator-fights, but they continued until the reign of Justinian. Martyr-acts provided a rival narrative spectacle, and where martyrs had died as part of Roman spectacle, martyr-stories re-enacted the deaths and re-valued them as triumph. Tertullian, deplorably, offered Christians the ultimate spectacle, the sight of those who had condemned and mocked them undergoing tortures in hell (*Spect.* 29). Prudentius wrote an allegorical poem, the *Psychomachia* (very popular in medieval culture), giving a blow-by-blow commentary on virtues defeating vices in gladiatorial combat (James 1999). Augustine recognised that his congregation felt the attraction of festivals, the theatre and the arena: he once preached for two and a quarter hours to keep them in church until the festival was over (*Ser. Mainz* 62), and he explicitly offered martyrs as a rival attraction. Why not be a martyr fan, he asked, rather than a charioteer fan? Christians were not the only people who attempted a rhetorical challenge to the games: a philosopher offered the spectacle of a man fighting to the death with fever, and the tutor of the future emperor Julian offered him Homer's account of chariot-racing. But martyrdom was much more exciting.

Traditional Romans were repelled by Christian interest in death and the dead. Philosophers offered advice on coping with pain and death, but their common ground was that death, pain and fear should be brought into perspective by reason, and that we should not encourage emotional or physical distress by giving it attention. Nor should we accept that pain is bad in itself: what matters is our response to pain, and that is always within our control. This seems a wildly optimistic assessment, even in a time when serious illness was likely to kill quickly and there were not many drugs that affected the mind. But Stoic philosophers assumed that there was always the choice of 'rational withdrawal', the decision not to continue living. The emphasis was on 'rational', for suicide prompted by emotional or physical distress was regarded as a failure of reason that might damage the soul: Plato offered the powerful image (*Phaedo* 67a) that we should stay at our post until dismissed by God. Philosophical texts, true to their principles, do not give detailed attention to physical suffering. They either mock excessive concern for minor troubles ('Oh dear, is it a bad cold?'), or try thought-experiments with dramatic examples of philosophers defying tyrants. A favourite example was Phalaris, the archaic Sicilian tyrant who roasted his victims in a hollow bronze bull, so that their screams sounded like the bull bellowing. In these extreme circumstances, could the Stoic wise man still be called happy? (The answer is that he could: see further Sorabji 2000.)

These texts do not dwell on suffering, but concentrate on the techniques of rational analysis and moral training by which the philosophically educated person can overcome suffering. By contrast, Christian texts narrate in detail the tortures permitted by Roman systems of punishment, in order to show how extremes of suffering can be transcended and given meaning. The *Passio Perpetuae* (15.6) says that Felicitas, the slave of Perpetua, gave birth to a daughter shortly before her execution. It was a difficult birth, and the prison guards asked her how she would cope with the far worse suffering to come. She replied 'What I am suffering now, I suffer for myself. But then another will be in me and will suffer for me, because I shall suffer for him.'

WHEN, WHY, HOW MANY?

Outbursts of hatred and mob violence, or denunciations by personal enemies, could happen at any time, especially at times of natural disaster, for example earthquakes (Cyprian, *Ep.* 75.1, mid-third century) and droughts. Such disasters had no obvious explanation, except that the divine powers in charge of the universe had been angered by Christian refusal to honour them. 'No rain: blame the Christians' became proverbial (Aug. *CD* 2.3). No rain meant no crops. Food shortage was a chronic problem (Garnsey 1999: 34–42), but if it could be blamed on Christians, the execution of Christians could defuse general anger, as in the martyrdom of Pionios (Robert 1994), and might even placate the gods.

It is not possible to say how many Christians fell victim to such attacks (Hopkins 1998): the numbers may have been in hundreds rather than thousands over three centuries. But, to use a modern analogy, it takes only one terrorist attack to make people afraid. Christian texts report that in time of persecution many people apostasised (literally, 'stood aside', that is, abandoned their faith). That may indicate a high level of fear in Christian communities; or it may indicate a relatively low level of commitment. The ancient world had nothing remotely like modern media coverage, but Christian churches passed on to each other their stories of heroic suffering, and commemorated the 'birthdays', that is the death-days, of their own martyrs by reading the stories. For example, the story of the martyrs of Lyon and Vienne was told in a letter from the churches in Gaul to their mother church in Asia Minor, and that letter was available to Eusebius (*EH* 5.1.3–63) well over a century later.

Charges against individual Christians usually depended on local enmity and popular feeling (ch. 2), and were not the result of imperial policy or of consistent repression. There are no reports of secret police hunting out Christians, and conscientious governors refused to accept anonymous denunciations. A few Christians deliberately attracted attention by going to the governor's tribunal to declare that they were Christian; a few refused to enter, or to continue, military service (see further ch. 6), because it entailed killing or because army ceremonial required worship of the empire's gods. There is no evidence for reprisals against their communities. In the second century especially, Christians had the confidence to write pamphlets addressed to the emperor, citing official documents that could be interpreted as legal protection for Christians, and asking for a response that would acknowledge the harmlessness of Christianity. This is one form of 'apologetic' (ch. 2), writing in defence of Christianity against actual or presumed attack. All Roman citizens were entitled to ask the emperor for an official response (rescript) on a legal question, but there are no extant rescripts addressed to the authors of these pamphlets, and here the argument from silence is very strong: Christians would certainly have made the most of them. So the pamphlets may have been open letters rather than formal requests, and such documents are usually more important to sympathisers, in this case members of Christian groups, than to those who need convincing. But they suggest at least that the Christian movement was not afraid to be noticed. Drake (2000: 85) sees the martyr and the apologist as representative of an internal tension in Christianity, 'the martyr standing for rigor and exclusion, the apologist for cooperation and inclusion'.

In the second half of the third century, the situation changed. For the first time, there were empire-wide edicts about religion and, at intervals, Christianity was directly targeted. In 249, the emperor Decius required all Roman citizens (that is, all free inhabitants of the empire) to sacrifice to the gods. There is no evidence that Jews had to sacrifice (Rives 1999: 138). Christian writers present this requirement to sacrifice as deliberate persecution, but Decius may have been more concerned, after years of ruinous civil war, to secure the goodwill of the gods and an affirmation of community. The edict might have been pious aspiration, but, remarkably, citizens were required to have a certificate stating that they had sacrificed. Fragments of almost fifty such certificates survive from Egypt, the only region of the Roman empire that had a climate likely to preserve them. Egypt was also the only region with enough bureaucracy to have any hope of issuing certificates to all who wanted them, by analogy with the local census (Rives 1999: 149). The standard form identified the person who requested certification and attested that he or she has always met his or her obligations. But what can Decius possibly have expected to happen in the great cities of the empire, Rome or Alexandria or Antioch or Carthage, with their immense and shifting populations and their very limited bureaucratic resources? Perhaps he did, after all, deliberately target Christians, by giving their neighbours an opportunity to put pressure on them.

There is very little evidence for what happened, with one exception. Carthage is the best-documented case of the 'Decian persecution', because the letters and treatises of Cyprian, bishop of Carthage, detail the attempts of his church to deal with varying responses to the edict. Cyprian, formerly a teacher of rhetoric, was an excellent preacher and writer, and his works were carefully copied and studied in Africa, especially in the disputes that followed the 'Great Persecution' of the early fourth century (see below). In Carthage, some Christians sacrificed, or at least took a token part in a sacrifice, and some acquired certificates without actually taking part. These Christians were referred to as 'lapsed' (Latin *lapsi*, 'fallen'). Some avoided trouble by moving away: they could cite in support the saying of Jesus 'when they persecute you in this city, escape to another' (Matthew 10.23). Others were imprisoned for refusing to sacrifice, and some died as martyrs. Some actually sought martyrdom, though the churches consistently discouraged this, on the grounds that self-sought martyrdom was evidence of pride not of faith (Bowersock 1995: 59–74).

Cyprian's problems were complicated by Christian 'confessors', so called because they had acknowledged their faith (see above). They could be visited in prison, and they issued their own certificates of reconciliation with those who had succumbed to pressure. They did not consult their bishop before doing this, perhaps because they thought (as in Perpetua's dream, above) that their spiritual authority as martyrs was greater than that of the church hierarchy, or perhaps because they wanted to show love and forgiveness before they died. Other hard-line Christians refused to be in communion with those who had denied the faith, certificate or no certificate, and the result was schism, a split in the church, both in Carthage and in Rome. (There was always a strong connection between Rome and the geographically close, Latin-speaking North African churches: Merdinger 1997.)

Cyprian at first thought it his duty to go into hiding so that he could continue to lead the church. Decius did not last long as emperor, but Cyprian was arrested and executed a few years later, when the emperor Valerian made a much more specific attack on Christians. The terms of this attack show the social spread of Christianity in the later third century.

According to a letter of Cyprian (80.1), Valerian ordered the punishment of bishops, priests and deacons. Senators and persons of rank were to lose their property and status, and to be executed if they persisted. Married women were to lose their property and be sent into exile; members of the imperial household were to lose their property and be sent in chains to work on the imperial estates. Cyprian's martyr-act (Musurillo 1972: 168–75) presents a courteous dialogue with the proconsul, in which Cyprian refuses to name his clergy on the grounds that imperial law bans informers. As one of the 'more respectable', the *honestiores*, Cyprian was beheaded, and the faithful spread cloths to collect his blood (see below).

Opponents of Christianity noted that the Christian God was apparently too weak or too unconcerned to protect his martyrs. The Christian author Lactantius replied that there was clear evidence of divine vengeance, for very soon after they instituted persecution, Decius became the first Roman emperor to die in battle and Valerian the first to be captured alive by the enemy (*De Mortibus Persecutorum* 2–5). Valerian's son Gallienus ended action against Christians, and confirmed by a rescript addressed to several bishops that occupiers should withdraw from places of worship and that the bishops could use the rescript against any interference; another rescript allowed bishops to recover cemeteries (Eus. *EH* 7.13). Gallienus lasted for fifteen whole years, an achievement for a third-century emperor. The emperor Aurelian, probably in 272, received a petition from Christians in Antioch about a dispute that affected possession of a church building. He assigned it, probably on their suggestion, to 'those to whom the bishops of the doctrine in Italy and Rome should write' (Eus. *EH* 7.30.19). Christianity, apparently, had become an accepted religious organisation, and according to Eusebius, the later third century was a period of peace and growth. There were Christian provincial governors, dispensed from the requirement to sacrifice; Christian families in the imperial household, openly practising their religion; and new, bigger church buildings in every city (*EH* 8.1).

Did this visible growth prompt the emperor Diocletian, in 303, to authorise the most serious episode of general repression, known to Christians as the Great Persecution? Once again, our sources are Christian. There were stories that oracles did not function, and divination at sacrifices did not work, because there were Christians present. When Christian courtiers made the sign of the cross at a sacrifice, their purpose was to protect themselves against demons (ch. 2) that might be attracted by the offering (Lact. *Div. Inst.* 4.27.1–5). But a pious pagan might interpret the sign of the cross as contamination of the sacrifice, because it symbolised a crucified man, an extreme case of the corrupt mortality that was incompatible with the presence of the gods.

Disrupted communication with the gods could have been a serious worry, especially for an emperor faced by the Sassanid Persian regime that had captured Valerian. The power to the east of the Euphrates was always a major threat to Rome, and the Sassanid rulers, who were much more formidable than their predecessors, had used the Zoroastrian religion to unite their territory. One reason for imperial action against the Manicheans (ch. 2) was that the movement came from Persia; Diocletian presumably did not know that Manicheans were also persecuted in Persia. His rescript against Manicheans (probably 302 CE) survives only in a comparison of Roman and Mosaic Law (*Collatio Legum Mosaicarum et Romanorum* 15.3; Lee 2000: 66) made by an unknown fourth-century author. Diocletian ordered the burning of Manichean leaders and their scriptures. Followers, unless they recanted, were to be executed and lose their property; anyone of rank was to lose their property and to be sent to the mines, a slower but inevitable death. Imperial action against Christians followed a similar pattern. Christian sources ensured that it had a very high profile, whereas few Manichaean sources survive (ch. 2). But the 'Great Persecution' is indeed remarkable in the history of Roman attitudes to non-Roman religion (ch. 1), in that it was a systematic attempt to eliminate a widespread religion, by demolishing its places of worship, burning its books, forcing its leaders to recant, and denouncing its beliefs and practices.

According to Lactantius (*Div. Inst.* 5.2–3), the first moves were ideological. A high-ranking official, Hierocles, argued in public lectures that the first-century philosopher Apollonius of Tyana performed more impressive miracles, and was a more admirable person, than Jesus of Nazareth (Swain 1999). A philosopher wrote an anti-Christian manifesto: scholars debate whether it was Porphyry (Digeser 2000: 5–6), who, according to Augustine (*CD* 19.23), cited oracles of Apollo and Hecate saying that Jesus was a wise man, but Christians were mistaken in worshipping him rather than learning from him about God (see ch. 6). Lactantius, writing his *Divine Institutes* in response to these attacks, knew that Scripture would not convince his opponents, so he argued from classical sources. His opponents had said that Christians rejected the inherited wisdom of philosophers and lawgivers: he replied that Christianity fulfilled their ideals, and therefore deserved toleration until its merits were recognised (Bowen and Garnsey 2003: 14–48).

At a lower intellectual level, Diocletian's colleague Maximin Daia circulated a document giving Pontius Pilate's version of the crucifixion:

They forged *hypomnēmata* ['notes' or 'minutes'] of Pilate and our Saviour, full of all kinds of blasphemy against Christ, and with the approval of their superior circulated them to every province under his control. Edicts required these to be posted publicly in every place, town and country, for all to see. Teachers were ordered to set them as lessons for the children to learn, instead of the usual lessons. (Eus. *EH* 9.5.1)

Another document repeated the usual scandals about Christian worship (ch. 2). Eusebius (*EH* 9.5.2) says that a *dux* (military commander) abducted some low-class women from the market place in Damascus, and forced them by threats of torture to say that they had once been Christian and could testify to Christian abuses. More positively, Maximin ordered the building of temples in every city and the restoration of sacred groves. For each of these he appointed priests who were expected to lead a visibly holy life, and high priests distinguished for their public service; this may have been a precedent for Julian (ch. 6, but see Nicholson 1994).

The stages of physical and legal attack are reconstructed from Lactantius and Eusebius. Lactantius says (*DMP* 12.1) that the attack began on the festival of the god Terminus, the boundary-marker. At dawn, the prefect arrived with officials and soldiers at the church in Nicomedia, a conspicuous building in sight of the palace. They broke in, looted and then demolished it, and burned the Scriptures. Next day, according to Eusebius (*EH* 8.2.4), an edict said that the same should be done everywhere. Christians of rank lost their civil rights, so were liable to torture. A token sacrifice was required before any appearance in a lawcourt, so Christians could not make use of the legal system. Christians in households lost their freedom: this probably means Christian civil servants who had been slaves in the imperial households. A further edict ordered that bishops should be imprisoned and made to sacrifice, and a later edict required everyone to sacrifice, although this cannot have been any easier to enforce than the edict of Decius half a century earlier. Different regions of the empire responded very differently. Christians suffered most in the territory controlled by Maximin Daia in the eastern Mediterranean. Eusebius narrated the appalling deaths of the martyrs of Palestine, his own country. In Alexandria there was schism, and one heart-breaking story tells of Christians in a prison cell rigging up a blanket to separate the two sides (Epiphanius, *Panarion* 68.3.3). But in Britain, governed by the father of the future emperor Constantine, and in Gaul, there is very little evidence for action against Christians (Thacker and Sharpe 2002).

North Africa is particularly well documented because events of 303 and after were used as ammunition in the long-lasting dispute that resulted from the persecution. The Donatists (named after a leader called Donatus) claimed to be the one true and faithful church, with authentic martyrs whose deaths were fervently commemorated (Tilley 1996). Other Christians, they said, were compromised directly or by association with those who had betrayed the faith. A century after persecution ended, Donatists were still in conflict with the church that claimed to be catholic (that is, universal, Greek *katholikos*). In 411 the imperial commissioner Marcellinus chaired a peace commission at Carthage, and many stories of the Great Persecution, including official documents, were read into the record (Edwards 1997; Lancel 2002: 293–300). Marcellinus was told how officials demanded that Christians should hand over their sacred texts. Some did hand over the Scriptures; some substituted other impressive-looking texts, such as medical books, that were accepted out of ignorance or, perhaps, reluctance to persecute; some refused and were imprisoned. Those who refused to hand over texts called the others 'handers-over', *traditores* or 'traitors', and argued that the *traditores* had betrayed the faith. Consequently, they said, *traditores* could not validly baptise, ordain to the priesthood, or consecrate as a bishop. This dispute became politicised in 313 when Constantine offered the churches financial support and restoration of property, only to discover that in Africa there were rival claimants for the title of the true church (ch. 6).

Persecution did not work. Christian writers praise the courage and endurance of Christians; other probable factors are general reluctance to act against Christians, indifference to the revival of traditional religion, and far too much else to worry about as a decade of civil war dragged on. The climb-down began in 311. Galerius, who was terminally ill, issued an edict saying that he had tried to restore ancestral tradition, but had found that many Christians, though frightened into quiescence, were neither worshipping the gods nor worshipping the god of the Christians. He therefore gave permission for Christians to 'exist again' and to rebuild their churches, provided that they did nothing against public order, and provided that they prayed for the emperor and the state (Lact. *DMP* 34.1–5). Then Constantine and his colleague Licinius, in 313, issued the declaration known (inaccurately) as the 'Edict of Milan' (ch. 6), which proclaimed general religious toleration for Christians and for others, and required Christian meeting-places and other church property to be returned to them free of charge. So persecution was over, and martyrdom at an end, except for Christian missionaries to dangerous places, and for Christian victims of religious disputes. But martyrs, and the imagery of martyrdom, then became even more important to the church (Markus 1990).

A HANDFUL OF DUST: MARTYRS AND RELICS

Martyrs were the church's heroes and its history, and their relics (Latin *reliquiae*, 'physical remains') were believed to have healing and protective power, as if the bodies that had shared Christ's acceptance of death were charged with spiritual force. The most extreme theological interpretation of relics, in a sermon preached by Victricius bishop of Rouen in 398, assimilates them to God, because the martyr is identified with the obedience of Christ, and Christ is God:

Perhaps, at this point, someone will cry out in protest 'Is the martyr, then, the same as the highest power and the absolute and ineffable substance of godhead?' I say he is the same by gift not by property, by adoption not by nature. (*Praising the Saints* 8; G. Clark 1999)

Religious concern for dead bodies, for bits of dust and ash, was a departure from Greek and Roman tradition. People were naturally concerned to show respect for their own dead, and for the spirits of the dead, but the divide between mortal humans and immortal gods was marked by purity rules: in Greek tradition all aspects of the mortal condition, including birth, caused religious pollution. Philosophers interpreted this religious tradition as expressing a truth about the mortal body in relation to the immortal soul, which escaped when the body died. Christian teaching on the resurrection of the body was especially hard for Romans to take (Bynum 1995). It was widely believed that the soul survived the death of the body, but why should it need the body, that so obviously did not survive? But authoritative Christian texts taught that Jesus Christ had died on the cross and had risen from the dead, not as a ghost or as a disembodied soul, but as a physical human being who could be touched and who ate ordinary food. 'Doubting Thomas' (John 20.24–9) would not believe that Jesus was alive unless he could actually touch his wounds: he was convinced. Paul argued (1 Corinthians 15.12–28) that the resurrection of Christ implied the resurrection of all Christians. The burial-places of Christian dead were called *koimētēria* (hence 'cemetery'), the Greek for 'sleeping-places': the sleepers would wake again in the general resurrection (Latin *resurrexi*, 'I have arisen').

Martyrs were thought to be early evidence for resurrection. The faithful believed that even the smallest fragment of a martyr's body, dust and ash, had the power to heal and protect. This power was taken as proof of continuing life: the martyrs were united with Christ in the love of God that had caused them to accept death, and were therefore united with Christ in his victory over death. The blood of martyrs had a special significance because blood was thought to be the basic stuff of life (ch. 4; G. Clark 1998a). 'Bloodshed' was used as a metonymy for all forms of martyrdom. Christians used cloths and sponges to collect the blood of a martyr, as they did when Cyprian died (see above), but any relic had power (G. Clark 2001b). Roman law usually allowed the bodies of condemned criminals to be removed for burial, or the bones and ashes to be removed if the execution had been by burning (*D.* 48.24.1), and these remains of martyrs were placed in memorial shrines. Christians also valued contact relics, such as clothes worn by the martyr, or even dust from the martyr's tomb: these too, some believed, were charged with the martyr's spiritual power. The Roman church, perhaps beset by especially high demand for relics, refused to distribute bodily remains, but offered instead strips of cloth that had been lowered through the protective grating to rest on the tomb of a martyr. Gregory the Great, bishop of Rome in the sixth century, was said to have authenticated such a relic: when Gregory cut the cloth, it bled (Thacker 1998: 66–7).

One story of the discovery of long-dead martyrs is especially informative. In 374 Ambrose, governor of Aemilia in North Italy (the region still called Emilia), was chosen as bishop of the regional capital Milan. The city was also an imperial capital, but that was a quite recent development in response to the threat of invasion through the Alpine passes. It had not been a major administrative centre in the centuries when Christians were persecuted, so, like Constantine's new capital Constantinople, it lacked martyrs (Humphries 1999). Ambrose set about transforming the city by building churches; friends in the East sent him relics of martyrs, and he placed them under the altars of his churches so that all could benefit from their power. He also shared them with friends in Italy and Gaul. Finally, in a difficult political situation (McLynn 1994: 181–208), he was directed by a vision to Milan's own martyrs, Gervasius and Protasius, who had died under Nero. Ambrose excavated in front of the screen that surrounded the grave of two other saints, who had been brought to Milan by a previous bishop. He reported (*Epistulae* 77 [22]) to his sister, who lived in a community of ascetic women (ch. 4), that he found huge bones, appropriate for men of ancient times, and much blood. Miraculous healings took place as the relics were moved to Ambrose's new church.

Ambrose thus provided Milan with strong spiritual protection and affirmed its heroic Christian history. We do not know what his political opponents said, but they could certainly have raised questions about what exactly he had found and whether he ought to have found it. Giants in the reign of Nero are improbable, but ancient heroes ought to have huge bones, like the bones of Orestes and Theseus that were moved in the late sixth and early fifth century BCE to protect Sparta and Athens respectively. Red stains on plaster may have been interpreted as blood, proof of continuing life. Ambrose noted that even his clergy had doubts about his excavation, and as a former governor, he knew that this disturbance of human remains was almost certainly illegal. 'Translation of relics' has become a technical phrase for ceremonially moving or distributing the remains of the holy dead: but *translatio* (Latin for 'movement') of the dead was forbidden by Roman law (G. Clark 2001b). Anyone who wanted to disturb a burial had to get official permission and to provide good reason, for instance that the burial-place was at risk from flood, or that the burial was only temporary and the final resting-place was now prepared. Ambrose could perhaps have used this argument, but he had not asked for a permit.

There was a further problem about moving the dead into cities. The city of Rome had a sacred boundary, the *pomerium*, so it was in principle a religious place in which the dead could not be buried. Many other cities had a similar tradition: this is why tombs are often found on approach-roads, such as the Via Appia. Christian churches were often located outside cities, and one reason for this is that they were often associated with burials, as in the case of St Peter's at Rome. Some more recently founded cities did not have this tradition against intra-mural burial, but in many places the transfer of martyr-relics to churches and shrines within the city might have been felt as an invasion by the dead (Markus 1990: 147–50).

The martyr Babylas, little known in his lifetime, illustrates the different perspectives on martyr-cult (S. Lieu 1989). This is the first known case of relic transfer. In the early 350s Babylas, entombed in his sarcophagus, was moved from a cemetery outside the walls of Antioch to the suburb of Daphne. There was an ancient oracle of Apollo at Daphne; it was also a favourite, and scandalous, resort for Antiochene high society. We do not know which of these facts motivated Gallus, a junior member of the imperial family, to have the body moved. When Julian, younger brother of Gallus, became emperor and renounced his Christian upbringing, he found that Apollo no longer gave oracles at Daphne, or indeed at Delphi itself. The last recorded Delphic oracle was a response to Julian's doctor Oribasius.

> Say to the king: the decorated court has fallen to the ground.
> Apollo no longer has a cell, or a prophetic laurel,
> Or a babbling spring: even the chattering water is dry.
> (*Anthologia Palatina* 3.6.122)

This was a blow, for Julian and others took oracles very seriously (ch. 5). But at Daphne there was an obvious explanation: the dead body of Babylas polluted the holy place, or, from a Christian perspective, the demon was silenced by the presence of the martyr. Julian had the body moved back. There were riots, and fire, whether of human or of divine origin, destroyed the shrine of Apollo. Eventually, the relics of Babylas were housed in a purpose-built, cross-shaped church.

There are no reports that anyone objected when Gallus first had the body moved. In general, the eastern churches saw no problem in moving martyrs and distributing their relics, for when a relic was divided, the donor lost nothing, and the gift united those who shared it. But Roman law on burial was another matter. In the year 357 the relics of Andrew the apostle and Luke the evangelist were transferred to Constantinople, another city that was short on martyrs, presumably with the consent of the emperor Constantius II (Mango 1990). In the same year, a law of Constantius reaffirmed the principle that the bodies of the dead must not be disturbed. He had on several previous occasions threatened heavy fines for anyone who removed building or decorative material from tombs: in 357 he added, again reaffirming tradition, that the same penalty applied to those who disturbed buried bodies or remains (*corpora sepulta aut reliquias*, *Codex Theodosianus* 9.17.4). It is not certain that he (or his legal advisors) intended also to restrict the movement of relics, but by the early 380s, Roman law explicitly connected martyr-cult with rules on burial. A law of 383, addressed to the prefect of Rome, restated the principle that bodies in sarcophagi or urns must be placed outside the city boundary, and added that apostles and martyrs were no exception. A law of 386, issued a few months before Ambrose excavated Gervasius and Protasius, restated the principle that it was not lawful to move bodies, and added that no one was to dissect or market the bodies of martyrs. But it was lawful to build a shrine at the tomb of a martyr, provided the tomb was undisturbed (*C. Th.* 9.17.7–8).

Roman law failed to prevent 'holy theft' of relics and disputes over the bodies of saints, and in the fourth and fifth centuries, martyr-cult became increasingly important. Martyrs became 'patron saints', taking the place of local protective deities and heroes (Brown 1981, MacMullen 1997). Human patrons could be asked to give immediate help or to use their influence at the imperial court; patron saints could be asked to give immediate help or to use their influence with the Almighty. Augustine, amongst others, found it necessary to explain that Christians did not pray to saints as if they were gods, but asked the saints for their prayers: his congregation may not have been as clear-headed about this as he was (*CD* 22.9; *De Cura* 6 with Trout 1999: 245). The commemorative shrines of martyrs were a focus for pilgrimage and for festivals that were sometimes dangerously similar to their 'pagan' predecessors. Girls were warned to stay close to their mothers, especially at vigils; people brought picnics and drank too much (Aug. *Epistulae* 29). It is also likely that Christian use of relics, for healing or for protection, seemed dangerously similar to some varieties of magic, which valued the body-parts of those who had died by violence (G. Clark 1999: 371–2). There is a splendidly sinister example of such magic in Apuleius (*Metamorphoses* 3.6).

Some Christians objected in principle to the cult of the dead. The most famous objection was quoted (or perhaps misquoted) by Jerome:

They take a pinch of dust, wrap it in a linen cloth, put it in a valuable container, and kiss it and venerate it. (Jerome, 4; Bynum 1995: *Contra Vigilantium* 92–4)

This protest came from Vigilantius, a priest from the diocese of Toulouse, who challenged both the cult of martyrs and the ascetic practices that often went with it. He may (Hunter 1999) have reacted against the extreme veneration of martyrs expressed by Victricius (above, and G. Clark 1999), whose sermon *Praising the Saints* was part of the official welcome to Rouen of relics sent him by Ambrose. Victricius reversed the roles of martyr and governor by describing the saints, fully present in their relics, as if they were governors, able to impose torture and punishment on the wicked (in this case, evil demons) and to instruct citizens on how they should live. When an emperor or his deputy made a formal arrival (*adventus*) at a city, the welcoming party would be the local civic leaders, and appropriate speeches would be made (MacCormack 1981: 17–61). Rouen's welcoming party for the relics, so closely connected to God, consisted of clergy and of ascetics, adorned with their virtues as a civic elite would be adorned with embroidered silks and jewels.

Asceticism, often called the 'long martyrdom' or the 'white martyrdom', deserves its own chapter (ch. 4). There were other ways of 'domesticating' martyrdom as a Christian way of life. In one of his recently rediscovered sermons, Augustine tries to shed the glamour of martyrdom on a man who wants to maintain post-marital celibacy (ch. 4; *Ser. Mainz* 42.2), and sternly resists the blandishments of parents and wife. (Was this a common pastoral problem in Hippo Regius?) Gregory the Great, in the sixth century, was prepared to equate 'carrying one's cross' with the faithful observance of holy days (Straw 1999). This seems like the beginning of the process described at the start of this chapter, the trivialising of martyrdom; but it also demonstrates the importance of martyrdom in early Christian self-awareness. Martyrdom could be reinterpreted as bearing witness to one's principles ('stand up and be counted') or as subordinating one's own will to the will of God.

CHAPTER 4

Body and soul

In their travels he came to a village, and a woman called Martha invited
him to her house. She had a sister called Mary, who sat at the Lord's
feet and listened to him. Martha, distracted by all the serving, came
and said, 'Lord, do you not care that my sister has left me alone?
Tell her to come and give me a hand!' But the Lord replied, 'Martha,
Martha, you are anxious and busy about so many things, but only one
is needed. Mary has chosen the better part, and it shall not be taken
from her.'

(Luke 10.38–42)

A man from a leading family asked him, 'Good teacher, what should
I do to inherit eternal life?' Jesus replied, 'Why do you call me good?
No one is good except God. You know the commandments: do not
commit adultery, do not murder, do not steal, do not give false testimony, honour your father and mother.' He said, 'I have kept all these
since I was young.' Jesus replied, 'There is one more thing that you
lack. Sell all you have and distribute the money to the poor, and you
shall have treasure in heaven, and come, follow me.'

(Luke 18.18–22; Mark 10.21 has 'take up the cross and follow me';
Matthew 19.21 has 'if you want to be perfect, sell what you have . . .')

RENOUNCING THE WORLD

In an Egyptian village church, at some time in the mid-third century, a
farmer called Antony heard the story of the man from a leading family.
According to his biography, he went straight out and sold his possessions,
established his sister in a community of Christian women, and himself
embarked on a solitary life of prayer and Bible study. The *Life of Antony*
does not ask why this, rather than mission or active charity, was his interpretation of 'come, follow me'. His fellow-villagers brought their problems to
this obviously holy man, so he retreated further and further into the uncul-
tivated land beyond the Nile valley. He learned the techniques of survival

60

for 'going up-country' (Greek *anachōrēsis*, which also means 'withdrawal', hence 'anchorite') that were probably developed to evade the demands of Roman taxation and Egyptian bureaucracy. Gradually, the Egyptian desert (*erēmos*, 'deserted land', hence 'eremite' and later 'hermit') acquired a population of monks (Greek *monachos*, 'solitary' or 'separate'), who lived alone or in single-sex communities.

By the mid-fourth century, stories of these 'Desert Fathers', their extreme austerity, and their spiritual power that defeated demons and healed illness, had spread far beyond Egypt (Gould 1993). Athanasius, bishop of Alexandria, publicised the *Life of Antony* in his various exiles to the West (ch. 6), and may have written an improved version (Brakke 1995); by 371 there was a Latin translation. The *Life* had a remarkable impact. In Trier (see below) two members of the imperial civil service found a copy in a household of 'servants of God', and abandoned their careers and their intended marriages. In Rome, the widowed aristocrat Marcella pioneered the monastic lifestyle in her own great house, with friends who lived enclosed in their rooms (Jer. *Ep.* 127.5). She received advice from Jerome, a brilliant product of Roman rhetorical education, who had also committed himself to the ascetic life, and who became its most outspoken publicist (Rebenich 2002).

In the late fourth century, Jerome was established in a monastery at Bethlehem. Its funding came from his friend Paula, another Roman aristocrat, who lived nearby in her own single-sex community (E. Clark 1986). When she died, he wrote to her daughter Julia Eustochium, in the expectation that his letter would be circulated and widely read.

Be confident, Eustochium: you are made rich by a great inheritance. The Lord is your portion, and – rejoice the more! – your mother is crowned by a long martyrdom. It is not only blood shed in confession of faith that counts: the service of a devoted mind is a daily martyrdom. The first crown is woven of roses and violets, the second of lilies. (Jerome, *Epistulae* 108.31)

Jerome assimilated Paula to the martyred heroes and heroines of the Christian church (ch. 3). In her lifetime, Christians were no longer executed for their beliefs, but she had chosen a lifestyle that testified to her faith. She had 'died to the world'.

Paula had made a suitable marriage at Rome. Widowed early, she made over her property to her children, arranged guardianship for her son, and sailed away to visit the monks of Egypt and the holy places of Palestine. Jerome describes how, on the quayside at Ostia, her little son stretched out his hands to her ship, and one of her daughters pleaded 'Stay for my wedding!' But Paula, despite her maternal distress, 'raised dry eyes

to heaven, overcoming devotion to her children by devotion to God'
(*Ep.* 108.6). Paula founded monasteries and gave so generously to the poor
that Eustochium, her companion, inherited only debts: hence Jerome's reference to her 'great inheritance', treasure in Heaven. Paula and Eustochium
lived in extreme austerity, praying and fasting. The early death of Paula's
daughter Blesilla, widowed soon after marriage, was ascribed to excessive
fasting (Jer. *Ep.* 39). Why did this form of asceticism seem to them, and
to Jerome, the right way of life for a committed Christian? How could
any Christian read the Gospels and conclude that what God really wants
Christians to do is to abandon their responsibilities to family and society,
starve themselves of food and human company, and even, in some cases,
refuse medical help or do themselves physical harm? The Gospels, and
other Bible texts, were read so as to support or to require the ascetic life
(E. Clark 1999); but the question is why anyone should want to read them
like that.

'Ascetic' comes from Greek *askēsis*, 'training', like the training of
athletes. The image of the spiritual athlete goes back to the letters of Paul
(1 Corinthians 9.24–7) and before him to Plato (*Republic* 403e). People
in training watch their diet and their lifestyle and fine-tune their bodies; in many traditions, they abstain from sex (though research before the
2000 Olympics suggested that this is not necessary). Spiritual athletes, as
the philosopher Porphyry put it, have entered the Olympics of the soul
(*Abst.* 1.31.3). But there were different ideas on the training of the spiritual
athlete (G. Clark fc a).

Philosophers urged their students to recognise that possessions are a
burden, and that greed and ambition only increase desire. The philosopher,
that is, the lover of wisdom, should cultivate detachment, reduce needs,
and remember that goodness, not success, is what matters. This is a sensible
technique for reducing stress, but it was more than that. Most philosophers
believed, with Plato (*Phaedo* 67a), that the needs of the body are a distraction
from the most important aspect of human life, the rational soul. This soul,
for them, was the defining characteristic of a human being, a 'rational mortal
animal' (on the assumption, rejected only by a few, that other animals are
non-rational: Sorabji 1993, G. Clark 2000a). Reason makes it possible for
us to understand the principles that govern the universe: it is our link to
God. But the soul cannot attend to God if the human being is preoccupied
with power or revenge or acquisition, or if the soul is distracted by the
body's demands for care. The preoccupations and the body's demands can
be minimised if they are brought under the control of reason, but some of
them cannot be ignored.

We have to eat, so twice a day for life, as the first-century philosopher Musonius Rufus said, we have to fight against gluttony and distinguish what we need from what we fancy. (The philosopher George Kerferd, a classicist of the later twentieth century, thought we should rather praise the dispensation of providence which ensures that, five hours after enjoying a good meal, we are quite ready to enjoy another.) Many philosophers, including Epicurus, advocated simple meals, because variety is expensive and stimulates appetite. Meat and wine, in particular, were thought to be over-stimulating. Some philosophers regretted the need to eat at all, for eating is a constant reminder of mortality: the soul is trapped in a decaying body that must be refuelled. But only Porphyry, in *On Abstinence* (G. Clark 2000a), comes anywhere near the extreme avoidance of food that some Christian ascetic texts display (T. Shaw 1998). Porphyry wrote in the later third century, probably too early for ascetic competition with Christian texts, but he displays some of the fantasies that contributed to late antique Christian asceticism. There was (and is) a recurrent fantasy of ascetic spiritual adepts, located in an exotic culture, who eat almost nothing. A recent example is a report of Zen Buddhist monks who supposedly exist on one small cube of tofu per week, because their metabolism is so perfectly in balance; similarly, the *Life of Antony* (14.3) claims that Antony, after years of rigorous fasting, was perfectly healthy. Porphyry's examples are priests of the ancient Egyptian religion, Essenes (borrowed from Josephus; ch. 2), and Brahmans.

Porphyry's ascetics belong to communities and follow a recognised lifestyle, but they spend much of their lives in silent contemplation, avoiding human contact. Brahmans, in particular, have to go away and recover if they are forced to talk to someone (*Abst.* 4.17.6). Porphyry advocates a solitary, celibate life for the philosopher: Augustine said that his slogan was 'avoid all body' (*omne corpus esse fugiendum*, *CD* 10.29). Here again Porphyry is unusual among philosophers, for most of them assumed that educated people can and should control sexual desire by reason. Food is necessary for life, but sex is not necessary, except for reproduction. So the only proper use of sex, they argued, is for the procreation of children within marriage; this is not, as is often supposed, a Christian innovation. Men should observe the same standards of chastity and fidelity that they expect of the women they marry. Non-marital relationships, heterosexual or homosexual, are an indulgence of lust, and every such indulgence makes it more difficult for reason to do its proper job of controlling desire.

'Should the philosopher marry?' was a well-worn lecture topic, not because marriage entails sex, but because marriage entails a household and children and all the distractions of family and social duties. But the answer was 'yes, he should marry' (nobody envisaged a choice for a female philosopher), because he owes grandchildren to his parents, citizens to his city, and worshippers to the gods. It was unusual for a Roman non-Christian male to abstain from marriage in order to lead the philosophic life. It is unknown for a Roman non-Christian female, with the one exception of Hypatia, daughter of the philosopher Theon, in late fourth-century Alexandria (Dzielska 1995). Philosophically educated Romans married and produced children, fulfilled their social and political duties, and lived modestly; given the chance, they withdrew to a country house and preferred *otium*, peace and leisure for studying philosophy, to *negotium*, 'non-leisure', that is, business. But they were not expected to abandon property, status and human company, and the responsibilities that go with them. Even the most austere versions of the 'philosophic life' were distinctively different from the lifestyle followed by the Christian 'servants of God' (G. Clark 2000b; see below).

Refusal to marry was also unusual, so far as the evidence goes (ch. 2), in Judaism of the early centuries CE. There is no suggestion in the New Testament that Jesus was married. Philo of Alexandria, writing *The Contemplative Life* in the mid-first century, described a celibate group called the Therapeutai (Taylor 2003), who, remarkably, included both men and 'elderly virgins'; Eusebius (*EH* 2.17) argued that this group was distinctively Christian. Josephus, writing after 70 CE, said that Essenes lived in a male single-sex community and adopted successors, but even among Essenes, some thought that marriage was required (*Bellum Judaicum* 2.160–3). This is a small number of examples, whereas celibacy was part of Christian tradition from the time of Paul's letters. Paul said that, although he had no 'word of the Lord' on the question, he thought it best for Christians to be as he was himself, not distracted by anxieties about spouse and children; but 'it is better to marry than to burn' (1 Corinthians 7.9). He did not mean by this that marriage is legitimate sex for those who cannot cope, but that marriage is a better option than being distracted by sexual desire. He also envisaged that some women might remain unmarried, or might choose not to remarry when widowed. By the second century, if not sooner, Christian communities had a recognised status for virgins and widows, and, if necessary, gave them financial support. Such women probably lived sheltered lives within households; communities of celibate women developed in the fourth century (Elm 1994), and the *Life of Antony* is probably anachronistic in saying that Antony, about 270 CE, placed his sister in a community of celibate women.

Celibate female communities were a new departure for Roman society and a new option for women; provided that it was really an option, and that the women were not under pressure from families who could not afford a dowry (Basil, *Epistles* 199.18) or who wanted the status conferred by a celibate woman (Cooper 1996). In traditional Roman religion (ch. 1), only a few cults required celibate priestesses, and life virginity was an even more unusual requirement. The Vestal Virgins, the best-known example, could in principle marry after thirty years' service, though tradition said that it never worked out; and, as Ambrose observed, Rome found it difficult to recruit even the necessary seven (*Ep.* 73.[18]11–12). The medical writer Soranus (early second century) noted in his *Gynaecology* (1.7.32) that life virgins were usually healthy, unless they got too fat from lack of exercise. He was interested because other doctors expected sexually inactive women to be unhealthy, but he did not say where he found his examples: perhaps in cults from his native Asia Minor (G. Clark fc a).

By the later fourth century, Christian advocates of asceticism said that life virginity was the best option for men and women. Celibacy, by agreement within marriage or after the death of a spouse, was the next best (though post-marital celibates were sometimes given credit for knowing what they were missing). Faithful married life was, too often, presented as a confession of weakness, and some writers expressed disgust for the messiness of childbearing and domestic life. Jerome was so outspoken on the subject that his friends tried to suppress a pamphlet he had written against Helvidius, one of the few known opponents of the ascetic movement. The silent majority mostly remained silent, continuing to marry and have children, and it is difficult to reconstruct the views of those who thought ascetic claims had gone too far: Vigilantius, Jovinian and Helvidius are known because Jerome denounced them (Hunter 1987). Opponents of asceticism could argue (according to Jer. *Ep.* 1.5) that it was Manichaean (ch. 2) in its prohibition of marriage and of many kinds of food, whereas Christians believe that God's creation is good, even if damaged by human falling away from God. They could also argue, in favour of Christian family life, that Mary gave birth to Jesus and was faithfully married to Joseph, and that the New Testament refers to brothers (possibly cousins) of Jesus. The resultant debate led to claims, eventually formulated as doctrine for some church traditions, that Mary, who according to current interpretation of Scripture had conceived as a virgin, remained virgin, that is, physically intact, during and after the birth of Jesus (Hunter 1993). In general, Christians who (unlike Jerome) had pastoral responsibilities were careful not to devalue marriage; even so, Ambrose and Augustine, Basil and John Chrysostom, were celibate bishops, and presented the celibate, world-renouncing ascetic life as the highest form of Christianity.

'WHERE DID ALL THIS MADNESS COME FROM?'

Celibacy, frugality, self-restraint, time for prayer and reflection, all have their value; there are people who need above all to pray undistracted; living in community is one of the great human social experiments. But how did it become possible for Christian writers to present life virginity as a triumph for women, when Roman society saw it as tragedy for a girl to die unmarried or a woman to remain childless? Why did some late antique Christians explicitly praise near-starvation, squalor, isolation, and in some cases self-harm, when Roman society valued prosperity and generosity to fellow-citizens, and Roman philosophical tradition valued simplicity and moderation?

In an influential set of lectures, published as *Pagans and Christians in an Age of Anxiety*, E. R. Dodds put the question starkly as 'Where did all this madness come from?' (Dodds 1965:34). Dodds, a classicist with a strong interest in psychology and the paranormal, suggested that neurotic concern about the individual body, which was not restricted to Christians, reflected anxiety caused by the political instability of the social body in the early centuries CE. This 'age of anxiety' (a phrase borrowed from the poet W. H. Auden) interpreted the material world as a place of exile or even imprisonment for the soul, so that the desires of the body distracted the soul as it worked to return to its true home (e.g. Plotinus, *Enneads* 1.6.8). The work of Mary Douglas on the anthropology of religion lent support to this correlation of social boundaries and body boundaries (Kraemer 1992: 13–21), which is exemplified by fourth-century interpretation of the intact virgin body as an image of the pure church, the bride of Christ (Brown 1988: 353).

There are other theories (discussed by Cameron 1986) that relate the development of asceticism to the condition of Roman society. The social historian Paul Veyne suggested, in an influential article published in 1978, that concern for oneself was a response of the Roman elite to the loss of political power: no longer able to control others, they tried to improve themselves, and invested much more in awareness of their responses and relationships. 'Concern for oneself' became a theme of Michel Foucault's even more influential history of sexuality in Graeco-Roman antiquity, published in the 1970s and 1980s. This work is not a survey of sexual behaviour or of sexual morality at different periods. It is an impressionistic and speculative account, often challenged by historians, of the ways in which people form themselves, and are formed by their society, as sexual beings, gendered beings, and more generally as 'subjects of their experience'. That means as people who do things and experience things, interpret their activity and experience, and reflect on what they should do. Foucault thought at first that there was a 'major break in sexual consciousness' (Cameron 1986: 266) in the nineteenth century. Exchange of ideas with the historian Peter Brown, a specialist in late antiquity, led him to see a new kind of subjectivity in Christian asceticism, and a new kind of repressive power in Christian discourse about sexuality. In his unpublished study of early Christianity, he was interested in Christian attention to sexual desire as the 'seismograph' of the soul (that is, as the manifestation of hidden turmoil), and in the practice of confessing desires, preferably in writing, as recommended in the *Life of Antony* (Boyarin and Castelli 2001).

Aline Rousselle (1988) suggested that asceticism reflected revulsion, especially women's revulsion, from arranged marriages, painful and unwanted childbirth, and modes of rearing children that made emotional relationships difficult (G. Clark 1994: 7–11). Peter Brown (1988), in a major study of sexual renunciation over the first five centuries CE, suggested more benignly that asceticism reclaimed the body, male or female, from the relentless purposes of Roman society. Christian ascetics rejected the obligation, recognised by most non-Christian philosophers, to perpetuate family and city. They did not (with a few exceptions) persecute the body for being an obstacle to the soul. Rather, their disciplines aimed to transform the body to fit the soul, so that body and soul could together respond to the will of God.

Asceticism continued to be intensively studied in the 1990s (e.g. Wimbush 1990, Wimbush and Valantasis 1995; Elm 1994, Grimm 1996, T. Shaw 1998), and much attention was given to the high valuation of virginity, and preoccupation with sexual desire, in Christian ascetic texts. This is another instance of social change affecting the concerns of scholarship. Popular versions of Freudian psychology drew attention to sexual desire, repression, and the need to confess one's desires. Sexual morality (or rather, publicly acknowledged sexual morality) was transformed by changing social roles for women and by the arrival of 'the pill' in the 1960s, and some late twentieth-century writing was just as earnest about working to enjoy sex as some ascetic texts were about working to renounce sex. In the western world, abundance of food led to preoccupation with exactly what food had what effect on the body.

Late antiquity, an increasingly fashionable field of study (ch. 1), provided some startling material about the interrelations of food, sex and gender roles. The opening chapters of the Bible (Genesis 1–3) presented the Fall, the separation of human beings from God, as the choice to eat forbidden fruit: the consequences were sexual awareness, gender roles (hard work for men and painful childbirth for women), dominance and desire in place of cooperation, and death. Could fasting and celibacy reverse these effects? Late antique theologians debated (E. Clark 1986) whether there was sex in Paradise, or whether sexual reproduction was merely damage limitation after the Fall brought death. Ascetics, living in celibacy, reported that fasting did not overcome the extraordinary persistence of sexual desire. Some were said to have practised fasting to an extent that is simply impossible, barring miraculous intervention or some unknown effect of endorphins: the human body just does not function on such low intakes of food and, especially, water (Grimm 1996). Rhetorical expertise provided dramatic and highly eroticised accounts of asceticism, most blatant when Jerome drew on the biblical Song of Songs to describe to Eustochium, daughter of Paula, how Christ the bridegroom comes to his bride (*Ep.* 122; P. Miller 1993): if you can sell anything with sex, does that include abstinence? Experienced ascetics discussed, explicitly but in discreet language, the problems of nocturnal emission (Brakke 1995) and sexual arousal; and some texts legitimise the revulsion from food, and from the mature sexual body, that is now classed as anorexia (Grimm 1996, T. Shaw 1998).

Most of these texts are addressed to women, but men were also encouraged to sexual abstinence and to extreme fasting, sometimes with an appeal to masculine superiority ('you can't let a woman beat you in spiritual athletics'), and sometimes with surprising rhetorical transformations of gender. Women ascetics could be upgraded to honorary men (Cloke 1995) because they had eliminated the physical and social femininity that made them inferior. It was more difficult to find imagery for men who overcame their physical and social masculinity (G. Clark 1998b), but there was praise for the 'manly eunuch' who had, in most cases metaphorically, become a eunuch for the kingdom of heaven's sake (Matthew 19.12; Kuefler 2001). Some texts praise the special beauty of the starved and de-sexed body that has lost male strength or female attractiveness and fertility.

This analogy with anorexia is a striking example of 'presentism', judging the past by the standards of the present. Historians, understandably, react against texts that appear to encourage an all too familiar kind of physical and psychological damage. But most present-day historians have no experience of, or sympathy with, Christian (and other) traditions of spiritual analysis and ascetic effort. Are they entitled to say that people who said they were dedicating their lives to God were really motivated by sexual anxieties they could not or would not recognise, and that there are obvious physical or psychological explanations for experiences that were (and in some traditions still are) interpreted as spiritual? For example: some recent victims of starvation have said that they wept whenever they spoke. This may provide an explanation for the puzzling 'gift of tears' that recurs in late antique ascetic texts: but constant weeping was prayed for as a gift because it could express constant penitence for the sins that separate the ascetic from God. Is an experience the same when it is enforced, whether by external or by internal compulsion, as when it is welcomed?

Similarly, it is argued that ascetics experienced as desire for God feelings that were 'really' sexual desire; but Plato argued that *erōs*, beginning as sexual desire, can reveal itself as really desire for God (Osborne 1994), and in Platonist tradition, that is the desire that reveals the true self. 'Looking within', in this tradition, is not preoccupation with one's individual characteristics or repressed anxieties. On the contrary, it is attention to the workings of reason that allow us to recognise our place in the universe and raise our minds towards God; Christian ascetics (see below) found it necessary to attend also to the thoughts that separated them from God. The philosopher Pierre Hadot (1995), writing on Platonist philosophy as a spiritual exercise, says that Foucault misinterpreted 'concern for oneself' as if it were 'a new form of dandyism', turning from the external world to take pleasure in oneself. Foucault is mistaken: the concern is for the true self that has not lost its connection with the divine power. On this interpretation, asceticism is not madness, but is a gradual recovery of sanity and spiritual health. But can health be recovered by the extreme methods reported and advocated in some late antique Christian texts?

The 'literary turn', characteristic of 1980s scholarship, has provided other possible answers to Dodds' question. One is that 'all this madness' would also have been regarded as madness in the fourth century, and therefore disregarded or given medical care, if Jerome and others had not written it up as holiness. All we have is texts: asceticism was hyped, and the most dramatic cases got the most attention. A stronger version of this argument is that accounts of extreme asceticism are not just exaggeration, but 'rhetoric all the way down': that is, they are not evidence for anyone who ever lived or anything that ever happened, other than for the text itself. But rhetoric is designed to persuade its target audience, so there is still a question why extreme ascetic practices could be presented as holiness, as the 'angelic life' of created beings who remain obedient to God. Even if they were only stories, 'armchair asceticism' (Philip Rousseau's phrase), why were these the stories people wanted (Cameron 1991: 89)?

The most plausible answers involve both the philosophical tradition that the body obstructs the soul, and the Christian history of martyrdom, which itself (ch. 3) connected with, and perhaps influenced, a preoccupation with the suffering body. After the end of persecution, how could Christians prove their commitment, and how could they share in the suffering of Christ and of the heroic martyrs? Christianity was perhaps too easy and comfortable since Constantine began to fund churches, and the 'super-Christians', the 'over-achievers' (Lane Fox 1986), needed a further challenge. One obvious challenge was to take the good news to the poor, feed the hungry, clothe the naked, visit prisoners and the sick, as Jesus told his followers to do (Matthew 25.35–41). Some Christians did indeed found hospices for the destitute and the sick, and some gave time and care as well as money (ch. 6). But the Christians who were held up for admiration went much further than cutting back their expenditure, or selling their surplus, to help the poor. Like Antony, they took Jesus' advice to the man from a leading family as addressed to them, and responded by abandoning worldly wealth and status.

ASCETIC METHODS

Why, then, the emphasis on fasting and on sexual abstinence? Some of the emphasis may be modern (see above) rather than ancient, and some of the reasoning may be strictly practical. Sexual desire leads to the commitments of family and society; acquiring and preparing food is expensive in effort and time; reduction in food intake, according to Roman medical theory, reduced fertility and the associated desires. Doctors correctly noted (T. Shaw 1998) that female fertility, and age at menarche, relate to food intake. A hardworking female slave would reach puberty later than an inactive well-fed girl; a female athlete or performer might stop menstruating at times of intense activity. The explanation offered was that food is digested ('cooked') into blood, and surplus blood is used for reproduction. Men have greater vital heat than women, so their surplus blood is further refined into semen, and they do not menstruate. (Difference in vital heat was a very useful theory. It also accounted for external male genitalia, superior male intelligence, and, according to Aristotle, male-pattern baldness.) So reduction of food intake would eliminate surplus blood, and with it fertility, and in due course desire. Recent studies of starvation confirm that there is rapid loss of libido.

Fourth-century ascetics found that escape from the demands of family and society can be very difficult to handle. Jerome wrote of his experiences in the mountains outside Antioch: the day stretched before him, he could fast, or pray, or read the Bible, or wait for his friend Evagrius to bring a fresh supply of books; and the empty landscape was filled with phantasms of dancing girls (*Ep.* 22.7). John Cassian, who trained in Egypt, described *akēdia*, the noonday demon (in cooler climates, it usually attacks nearer 4 p.m.), a condition in which everything seems unrewarding, and the ascetic becomes convinced that the only solution is to be somewhere else with different people. Ascetics needed work, physical or spiritual; a structure for the day; and a basic rule of life that could be adapted to individual strength. In Egypt, some wove palm-leaf baskets to sell for subsistence food and to provide for the poor. Pachomius founded communities whose members farmed the 'desert' land: they were self-sufficient and provided a surplus for the poor, because they were not supporting families (Rousseau 1985).

Community rules developed in the later fourth century, when collective experience showed their advantage over individual decisions on what to eat and how to live (Gould 1993). In the Egyptian desert of Scetis, most ascetics lived in community, and only those who were spiritually most advanced were thought capable of going solitary. Augustine's rule, for communities of men or women, may be the earliest surviving example (Lawless 1987); it is still fundamental for the Order of Saint Augustine. Basil's rule, the foundation of monasticism in the Greek Orthodox church, began as a set of authoritative responses (rather like imperial rescripts) to questions from the communities he founded in Cappadocia (Rousseau 1994). 'Monasticism' is a paradoxical word, in that Greek *monachos* (hence 'monk') means 'solitary'; communities of 'solitaries' living in a *monastērion* ('place of solitude') are distinctively Christian (see below). As Basil pointed out, Christians are supposed to show love for their neighbours, and they can scarcely do so when they live alone; moreover, where there is system and support, neighbours in need can be helped more effectively, and monks can still have time for prayer. A monk should not strip off his one garment to clothe the naked, but he should go to the monk who is in charge of distributing clothes.

Augustine provides a range of examples of western asceticism (C. Harrison 2000: 158–93). In *Confessions* (8.6.14–15) he tells a story that was told to him by a high-ranking civil servant, Ponticianus, whom he knew in Milan in the 380s. When the imperial court was at Trier, Ponticianus and three colleagues went for a walk outside the walls. Two came upon a house where 'servants of God' lived, and found there a copy of the *Life of Antony*: they decided to renounce their careers and become servants of God themselves, and their fiancées followed their example. Ponticianus and the other colleague continued their careers, but with great sadness. This story was one of the factors in Augustine's own liberation (for so he saw it) from ambition and from sexual desire. He too abandoned his career as a teacher of rhetoric and the marriage that had been arranged for him, and began a celibate life of prayer and study. The first phase of this life was spent at a country house, lent to him by a friend, where he and some students and relatives lived simply, discussing philosophy and literature: this was traditional *otium*, cultivated leisure, with the addition of Christian scripture, especially the Psalms. *Confessions* does not discuss the option of joining a monastic community at Milan (*Conf.* 8.6.15) or at Rome, but when Augustine returned from Italy to Africa, he lived in a community of like-minded friends on the family land at Thagaste. These 'servants of God' aimed *deificari in otio*, literally to 'be made god in freedom from busi-ness': 'assimilating to god' was Plato's phrase for what philosophers should do with their lives (Russell 2004). When Augustine was forcibly ordained priest at Hippo Regius, he continued to live in a single-sex community in a house that belonged to the church (Lancel 2002: 224–5).

Jerome's experiments in asceticism were very different (Rebenich 2002). On his own account, he was an earnest young man, who used to visit the catacombs on Sunday walks in Rome. He was baptised, and, some years later, tried out various forms of the ascetic life, first in north Italy and then in Palestine. He made acerbic comments on ascetics who invent their own mode of life and support themselves by selling overpriced craftwork (*Ep.* 22.34.2). In later European tradition, it was his time in a cave in the Syrian desert that painters found irresistible. They depicted Jerome lamenting his sins among the rocks, accompanied only by a patient lion (who had migrated from the story of Saint Gerasimos); a wide-brimmed red hat, such as cardinals wore centuries later, indicated his (brief) connection with bishop Damasus of Rome (ch. 5). But the cave, on the evidence of Jerome's letters, had a lavish supply of books and a staff of helpers. Friends came out from Antioch, and fellow-ascetics came to visit. The Syrian desert, like the Egyptian desert, had patches of cultivation, and hermits who spent much time in solitude also found solace in visiting and news (Gleason 1998).

Jerome encountered some strange forms of asceticism: one man had spent thirty years enclosed, living on coarse barley bread and muddy water, and another lived in a dry water-cistern, eating only five dates each day. But he found that his fellow-ascetics, so far from inspiring him with examples of holiness, were given to theological polemic. The extraordinary Syrian ascetic tradition was later described more fully by Theodoret (*Historia*

Religiosa, mid-fifth century), who did not approve of all its manifestations. One man was weighed down by chains, another ate grass. Such behaviour could be interpreted (as the twentieth-century psychologist R. D. Laing interpreted the behaviour of some patients) as acting out the condition of human life experienced by these people. Thus chains might symbolise the constraints of sin; grass-eating might be a reversion to primitive life, or perhaps a reference to the madness that afflicted King Nebuchadnezzar, who ate grass (Daniel 4.30). Syria was also the home of stylite saints, who took up residence on pillars (Greek *stulos*), perhaps following a local tradition of worship (Lane Fox 1997). The most famous case is Simeon Stylites (Doran 1992), who built his pillar ever higher, perhaps to avoid the importunity of visitors, perhaps to come closer to heaven. He had (as it were) surgery hours for consultation, but otherwise devoted himself to prayer. He was exposed to extremes of heat and cold, and his legs became gangrened.

It is easy to react with horror to this apparent waste of a life: but, as in the case of Roman reactions to the deaths of martyrs, there are other possible interpretations. To a disciple of Simeon, the maggot that fell from a wound in Simeon's leg was a priceless pearl.

When we look at Simeon from our modern point of view, we see a brutal life of self-inflicted pain. When his contemporaries looked at him, they saw a life transformed, a man transfigured, a world redeemed. This was not a mass hallucination. They saw these things because they saw them concretely enacted. Simeon lived the life he did and it did not kill him; at his pillar the sick were healed, the hungry were fed, the down-trodden were championed. (Harvey 1992: 11).

Ascetics such as Simeon devoted their lives to bringing down the barriers that separated them from God. Their techniques of solitude and fasting and endurance of self-imposed pain continued through centuries of Christian tradition. Few present-day Christian religious would endorse those techniques, but there are still people who experience the vocation to a form of the religious life that gives them the time they need for prayer.

For some, prayer is their contribution to the needs of the world, just as Antony, facing demons alone in the desert, was understood as the front line of resistance to an evil power. Simeon gave some time, carefully limited, to dealing with the needs of others; some stories of the desert fathers show tact and affection and disregard of self in relation to fellow-ascetics and to visitors (R. Williams 2003). But many stories of Christian ascetics, starting with the *Life of Antony*, show their hero running away from 'spiritual tourists' with their distracting demands for practical or spiritual help, especially from women who might prompt desire:

'Have you not heard of my way of life, which ought to be respected? How dare you make this journey? Do you not realise that you are a woman and cannot go just anywhere? Or have you come so that you can go back to Rome and say "I have seen Arsenius"? They will make the sea into a highway with women coming to see me.' She said, 'Please God, I will not let anyone come here; but pray for me and remember me always.' He replied, 'I pray God to take the memory of you from my heart.' (Arsenius 28, 65.96)

There are also stories that praise ascetics for rejection of family. The most appalling example, narrated by Cassian (*Inst.* 4.27), is the man who proved that he had a vocation to be a monk by his indifference to his fellow-monks' mistreatment of his eight-year-old son (see further G. Clark 1994). Basil and Augustine show more sense, saying that people who have family obligations are not free to lead the ascetic life.

'Holy men' who lived in solitude might still be important to a local community. An influential early paper by Peter Brown (1971) discussed their role as patron and as trouble-shooter, especially in the contexts of Syria and Gaul. The twenty-fifth anniversary of this paper prompted two collections of responses (Elm 1998; Howard-Johnston and Hayward 1999) including Brown's own reflections on its origins. These collections illustrate different ideals of the holy man in different contexts, but the most far-reaching change in the twenty-five years is emphasis on the holy man constructed, rather than reported, by the texts: why was resistance to society presented as an ideal?

THE PHILOSOPHIC LIFE

The contrast between Christian and non-Christian asceticism, in methods and in relation to society, is shown by two exemplary accounts of the philosophic life written in the late third or early fourth centuries. Porphyry's *Life and Writings of Plotinus* (Edwards 2000) was an introduction to the writings that Porphyry had edited and reorganised into Enneads (sets of nine). This new edition, completed in 301 or later, may be connected with other philosophical challenges to Christianity before the 'Great Persecution' (ch. 3). Porphyry's Plotinus comes from somewhere in Egypt, is celibate, lacks possessions, eats a frugal vegetarian diet, and sleeps little. He leads this simple life in the house of a Roman lady whose husband may briefly have been emperor. Anyone, according to Porphyry, could come to hear Plotinus, but the students he mentions were all educated professionals, and the *Enneads* are philosophically demanding. Plotinus wanted to live in a philosophical community, Platonopolis (O'Meara 2003), but the promised imperial funding was withdrawn. In Rome, he did his social duty, agreeing to arbitrate in legal disputes and to be trustee for fatherless children. He was a conscientious trustee, for unless the children grew up to be philosophers, he said, they were going to need the money. Porphyry argued in *On Abstinence* (see above) that the true philosopher should withdraw from all social contact, but he too fulfilled social duties. He married the widow of a friend, who needed support because she had children and was not in good health, and he had family property (G. Clark 2000a).

Iamblichus, a younger contemporary of Porphyry, ascribed his version of the philosophic life to the archaic sage Pythagoras, whom he presents as both a religious genius and a profound philosopher. His Pythagoreans live in a separate community at some distance from their city; they live in families, but have their possessions in common; their daily life has a structure of contemplation, discussion, and meetings for meals. Pythagorean teachings are accessible to busy, or to simple, people in the form of maxims, but their hidden meaning is profound enough to occupy the most intellectual. At least some Pythagoreans devote part of the day, after lunch, to the administration of the city. Iamblichus himself, and his students, fulfilled their own social and civic duties: they married and held public office (Fowden 1982).

These are different versions of the philosophic life, but they share differences from Christian asceticism (G. Clark 2000b). They are intended for the highly educated who have private funds, whereas Christian asceticism was accessible to the poor and uneducated. Philosophers were expected to live simply, but not to abandon their wealth or status. The Pythagoreans described by Iamblichus wear pure white linen, so that they are always ready to offer sacrifice; Christian ascetics wore black, because coarse dark cloth was cheap. 'Changing one's clothes', from the embroidered silks of the rich to the dark haircloth of the lower orders, the *humiliores*, was a recognised signal of Christian ascetic commitment. 'Humility', literally 'lowliness', is a distinctively Christian virtue, inspired by recognition of the humility of Christ (Lact. *Div. Inst.* 4.26.30). It is unfashionable, because it is easily confused with refusal to acknowledge that one has abilities. (That is not a Christian virtue, as Jesus' parable of the talents made clear: Luke 19.11–25.) Humility began in a Roman society that treated *humiliores* not only with contempt but with legalised violence (ch. 3), and in that context, humility signalled the unimportance of worldly status in awareness of the overwhelming greatness of God. Thus (ch. 5) a highly educated Roman of excellent family might be a mere beginner in comparison with an Egyptian peasant. Humility did not signal identification with the poor, or a commitment to live and work among the poor. But Christians were expected to care for those in need, and the philosophic life had no such requirement. Christian ascetic preaching can be seen as Plato democratised (ch. 5), a late-antique 'ascetic mentality' (Markus 1990) exported from the educated elite and presented to ordinary Christians. On the positive side, asceticism offered an alternative to the demands of family and social life, and ascetic communities made provision for the poor. On the negative side, ascetic preaching may have made some people feel inferior about their concern for family and social life, and may have pressured others into a life they experienced as deprivation.

Does late antique asceticism manifest a more general shift in human consciousness? Christian ascetics were encouraged to look within themselves, not, as in Platonic philosophy, to reflect on the workings of reason and thus to ascend towards God, but to detect the hidden thoughts and persistent desires that separated them from God. Sexual desire was a particular concern, because its physical manifestations were a constant reminder that in fallen human beings, the body does not respond to the control of reason, and may betray desires that are below the level of consciousness. Christian ascetics were therefore encouraged to confess such desires, to a spiritual mentor or in writing, whereas the philosophical tradition was to give them as little attention as possible. Perhaps these differences add up to a different interpretation of what it is to 'know yourself'. On the temple of Apollo at Delphi, 'know yourself' probably meant 'know yourself to be mortal'; in most philosophical traditions, 'know yourself' meant 'know your true self to be your immortal rational soul'. Some advice offered to Christian ascetics suggests that 'know yourself' meant 'know your desires'.

Large-scale conclusions have been drawn from these differences. Late antiquity has been credited with a new sense of self, even with the discovery of the individual (which has also been dated to several other periods of history) as distinct from the self that is defined by social context and performance of social role (Cooper 1996: 144–7). 'Only in the private reflection of a Christian before God did a modern individualism become conceivable at all' (Swain 1997: 8). But as early as the end of the fifth century BCE, Plato, the philosopher whose work especially influenced late antiquity, urged his readers to define themselves not in relation to society, but in relation to God. If there was a distinctive Christian sense of self in late antiquity, one factor is the distinctive language of prayer provided by the Jewish scriptures, above all by the Psalms. Greek and Roman literature has nothing comparable to these first-person songs of praise and reproach and appeal to God.

Other factors are the distinctive Christian doctrines of incarnation and resurrection, which insist that divinity and humanity, immortal and mortal, are not incompatible. Augustine remarked (*CD* 10.29) that the doctrine of incarnation is not as difficult as Platonists claim, for the union of God and human in Christ is no stranger than the union of body and soul in every human being. The resurrection of the body was even more puzzling (ch. 3; Bynum 1995): it was much easier to think in terms of the soul inhabiting a recalcitrant mortal body that would eventually be discarded. But, Augustine said, the body would not be a problem if the soul had not made it so: it is not the corruptible body that made the soul sinful, but the sinful soul that made the body corruptible (*CD* 14.3). Both can be redeemed and transformed, so that even the body can live with God; the 'resurrection body' may differ from the body of this life as much as the ear of corn differs from the seed-corn (ch. 3).

Why did Christian asceticism become so much more extreme than philosophic asceticism? Perhaps because Christian ascetics were working to transform body as well as soul; perhaps because they identified with the suffering of Christ and of the martyrs. Or perhaps historians are working with rhetoric 'all the way down' and should acknowledge that they cannot say anything about the experience of the people whose Lives and Sayings they read, but can discuss only representations and constructs. If so, it remains important that these are the representations and the constructs that some late antique Christians found worthy of admiration.

CHAPTER 5

People of the Book

Jesus came to Nazareth, where he grew up, and, as was his custom, went to synagogue on the Sabbath, and stood up to read. He was given the book of the prophet Isaiah, and, opening it, found the place where it was written, 'The spirit of the Lord is upon me, for he has anointed me to proclaim the good news to the poor. He sent me to declare release for captives, sight for the blind, release for the oppressed, to declare the Lord's year of favour.' He closed the book, gave it to the attendant, and sat down. The eyes of all in the synagogue were fixed on him. And he began his address to them, 'Today this scripture is fulfilled in your hearing.'

(Luke 4.16–21)

The proconsul Saturninus said, 'What do you have in your case?'
Speratus said, 'Books and letters of Paul, a just man.'
The proconsul Saturninus said, 'Take a reprieve of thirty days and think it over.'

(*Acts of the Scillitan Martyrs*, 180 CE)

CHRISTIAN LITERACY

The proconsul Saturninus, seeing that the accused had a *capsa*, a scroll-box, dutifully checked whether it contained material relevant to the trial. What exactly did the martyr Speratus reply? Latin *libri*, here translated 'books', may be 'the books', Greek *biblia*. (*Biblia*, an alternative spelling of *bublia*, is the plural of *bublion*, 'a strip of papyrus'.) That is, it may be the Bible, the scriptures (Latin *scriptura*, 'writing'), whatever that meant to a group of North Africans in the late second century. The canon of scripture (Greek *kanōn*, 'rule' or 'standard'), that is, the list of authoritative writings, took some time to be established (Layton 1987: xix–xxi). Speratus may have brought gospels, or some of the Jewish scriptures (ch. 2), especially those that Christians interpreted as foretelling Christ. The important point is that he had brought books, because they were central to his religious beliefs. He may have hoped for a chance to explain. If so, his explanation is not included in the account of his martyrdom. This martyr-act (ch. 3) sometimes keeps closely to the terse style of a court record (see T. Barnes 1985: 262–3 for problems of procedure), and here it moves on to the next essential point: the accused should be offered time to reconsider.

We do not know about the social and educational level of Speratus and his companions, but at least one of them could read. There are very varied estimates of literacy levels in classical antiquity. Most of the evidence, as so often, comes from Egypt, where many documents record 'I have written this for him/her, because s/he does not know letters.' Harris (1989) suggests that Roman culture had a literacy rate of 10 per cent at most. Did Christians have above-average literacy rates, because texts were so important to them? In the early centuries CE, the codex, that is the book, gradually took over from the scroll. It used to be argued that Christians preferred codices, because they wanted to differentiate their scriptures from the scrolls of the Jewish law, or for the practical reasons that a small codex is easier to carry than a scroll and that it is easier to find references in a codex. This argument for specifically Christian use of codices depended on a small number of examples from Egypt, and further discoveries have changed the statistics (Gamble 1995: 49–66), but Christian use of texts is not in doubt. They had scriptures, they kept in touch by letters, and the letters they exchanged not only gave local news (for instance, of martyrs, ch. 3), but offered exhortation and discussed doctrine and practice. Christian writers elaborated new versions of the gospels, and exciting new stories about the apostles that often resemble ancient novels (Bowersock 1994, Goldhill 1995). Some of these texts, excluded from the canon, are classed as apocrypha (Greek for 'hidden' or 'secret') or, in another recent change of terminology, as parabiblical literature. Christians also developed set forms of prayer, called liturgy (from Greek *leitourgia*, literally 'work of, or for, the people'), and some of these were recorded in texts, though it is very difficult to date the different phases of a diverse tradition (Bradshaw 2002). Debates about heresy and orthodoxy and statements of Christian belief focussed on the exchange of texts: it would have been difficult to define acceptable and unacceptable beliefs without them. Christianity (as always, without sharp distinction from Judaism) was distinctive among the religions of the Roman world in its level of attention to texts (ch. 2).

One example is the development of the creed, the statement of Christian belief. 'Creed' comes from Latin *credo*, 'I believe', the first word of most creeds, but Christians in the early centuries used the Greek word *sumbolon*, 'token of identity' or 'password'. Thus Ambrose, *De Symbolo* is the text of Ambrose taking a baptism class through the creed in Milan in the late fourth century: he told them to learn it, keep it secret, recite it to themselves, and it would keep them safe and well. Christians were not alone in having *sumbola* (ch. 2), but the Christian *sumbolon* developed into a statement of belief in several clauses, and the creeds that were agreed by church councils, from the fourth century on, also denounced mistaken beliefs. Eusebius, for example, wrote to his church (Socr. *EH* 1.8) explaining his attitude to the creed accepted at the Council of Nicaea and to the concluding statement that 'anathematized' anyone who used any formula implying that Christ was a created being.

'Let him be *anathema*' means 'let him be accursed'. It is likely that, as in present-day discussions on ecumenism or liturgical reform, only a small number of Christians were seriously concerned about precise forms of words. But those few succeeded in excluding from communion, and sometimes from the Roman empire (ch. 6), Christians who formulated their beliefs in unacceptable words. This was remarkable. Roman religious ceremonial often required exactly correct recitation of a traditional prayer, but neither 'civic' nor 'elective' Roman cults (ch. 2) excluded worshippers because of the words in which they formulated their religious beliefs. Philosophers disagreed about the correct interpretation of Plato, and their arguments against those who diverge from the truth may have been a factor in the Christian search for shared orthodoxy (Boys-Stones 2001). But there is no philosophical parallel for Christian 'heresy lists', beginning with Irenaeus in the mid-second century, that name heresies as if they were identifiable diseases. The most striking example of these lists is the 'medicine chest' (*Panarion*) of Epiphanius, written in the late fourth century and identifying as many heresies as King Solomon had concubines.

Roman religion, and philosophical debate, also had no equivalent of the Christian doctrinal violence that broke out when the words became slogans and the theological debates became assertions of support for one group rather than another (ch. 6). Some theologians tried to explain their position in popular terms. Arius used the catchy metre of comedy (R. Williams 2001: 99); Augustine wrote an 'alphabet song' against Donatists, saying 'I wanted even the humblest and wholly uneducated to know about Donatism, and to do all I could to fix it in their memory, so I wrote a psalm for them, going through the letters of the Latin alphabet': *Retractationes* 1.20.) These uneducated supporters were probably illiterate: how many could have explained exactly what they were singing about? Gregory of Nyssa complained about ignorant use of theological slogans in Constantinople in 381:

Ask, 'Can you give me change?' and they talk philosophy about the Begotten and the Unbegotten. Ask, 'What's the price of bread?' and they reply, 'The Father is greater, and the Son is subject to him.' Ask, 'Is the bath ready?' and they affirm that the Son has his being from the non-existent. (*On the Divinity of the Son and the Holy Spirit, PG* 46: 557; for context, Lim 1995: 149–81)

In Milan at this time, the labels 'Arian' and 'Catholic' (ch. 1) marked political as well as theological allegiance; a century later in Gaul, they identified followers of rival kings who had different traditions of theology.

Even if few Christians were theologically expert, they had reasons to be text-minded, and therefore a motive to be literate; but there are many forms of literacy (Gamble 1995: 2–10). There is high-level literacy like that of people who read this book, basic literacy that allows people to spell through a familiar kind of document, and functional literacy that allows them to recognise an important notice. Texts can be of central importance provided that everyone in a group knows they matter and at least one person can read. In the Roman world, texts were written in the expectation that they would be read aloud and shared with a group. This is why Augustine makes a point about Ambrose reading silently and with total concentration: he does not mean that silent reading was unknown (*Conf.* 6.3.3, with O'Donnell 1992: II.345). A literacy rate approaching 10 per cent is shockingly low by modern standards, but it is still a lot of people who can read (Hopkins 1991).

SIMPLICITY AND STYLE

Christians had reason to be literate, but their opponents claimed that they were uneducated. Even in the early fifth century, Augustine met social and intellectual snobbery: 'Am I to be what my concierge [*ostiaria*] is, not what Plato and Pythagoras were?' (*Ser. Mainz* 62.59). Celsus (ch. 2), writing against Christianity in the mid-second century, said that it was spread by the most ignorant people, those who had only the most basic skills. Wool-workers, cobblers, laundry-workers, and illiterate peasants get into private houses; they would not open their mouths in front of the master, but they tell children who have 'stupid women' (probably slave nurses) with them that they must disregard their father and school-teachers, and obey them instead (Origen, *C. Cels.* 3.55). Origen, replying to Celsus a century later, responded by challenging the teachings advanced by fathers, schoolteachers and philosophers.

Jesus thanked God 'for hiding these things from the clever and revealing them to the simple' (Matthew 11.25). The word here translated 'simple' is *nēpios*, which also means 'small child', and Christians who were baptised as adults were encouraged to think of themselves as newborn, in need of the most basic education (G. Clark 1994: 25–6). One way of countering the charge that Christians were uneducated was to devalue formal education, and this was often done by Christians who, like Origen, were highly educated. They could claim that Christian simplicity surpassed philosophy, for everyone knows that philosophers cannot agree about anything important and spend their time tying each other up in verbal knots. Philosophy, Augustine said, was Babylon, the city of confusion (*CD* 18.41); philosophers could counter that Christians disagreed among themselves and diverged from the common tradition (below, and Boys-Stones 2001: 152–3.) Stories of the 'desert fathers' (ch. 4) showed that illiterate peasants could have deeper understanding than the best the Roman world could offer:

'Abba Arsenius, how is it that you, with such a good Roman and Greek education, ask this rustic about your thoughts?' ['Thoughts' in this context means distracting thoughts or desires.] Arsenius replied, 'I have had a Latin and Greek education, but I have not learned the alphabet of this rustic.' (Arsenius 6, *PG* 65.89a)

Arsenius, before he chose the ascetic life in the Egyptian desert, had been tutor to the sons of the emperor Honorius (early fifth century CE). The 'rustic' would be assumed not to know the alphabet of Latin or Greek, perhaps not even to speak the language.

These stories of simplicity were told by and for sophisticated people (Cameron 1991). Christians were often accused of relying on faith rather than reason; thus Galen (ch. 2) contrasted his own use of demonstration with his medical rivals who expected to be believed without proof, like 'the school of Moses and Christ' (Wilken 2003: 72). In practice, Christian attitudes to philosophical argument varied. An opponent who engaged in it, especially an opponent who seemed to be winning, might be accused of disregarding fundamentals from sheer love of disputation (Lim 1995), just as people today are accused of making merely academic points. But there were also Christians who argued that Christianity is the true philosophy (see below), and there were some who engaged in very technical disputes, using all the resources of philosophy, about the humanity and divinity of Christ and the relationship of God to the world (Stead 1994). Many Christians used or dismissed philosophy according to need. For example, Ambrose of Milan had an excellent education, and could easily adapt in Latin complex philosophical argument by his Greek-speaking contemporary Basil of Caesarea, another highly educated bishop (Rousseau 1994). Ambrose was quite capable of attacking 'dialectic', that is, philosophical argument, in a sermon that made use of dialectic. Another favourite tactic was to begin an argument, then sweep away the debate as irrelevant to faith, as Victricius of Rouen did in his sermon on relics (ch. 3): 'I am not tied in the tangle of hypothetical and categorical syllogisms; the empty sophisms of philosophers do not deceive me. Truth herself reveals her face, and faith spurns arguments' (*Praising the Saints* 11, tr. G. Clark 1999a: 394).

Christian attitudes to rhetorical skill also varied. Augustine, in some contexts, acknowledged that the apostles were poor and uneducated men, and argued that the spread of Christianity, against all the odds, was further proof that it was God-given. But in other contexts he presented Paul as a master of rhetoric, and used Paul's letters to demonstrate that Christians could pick up the basics of rhetoric just from reading or hearing the scriptures (*De Doctrina Christiana* 4.31–45): they did not need an expensive education, such as Augustine himself had both received and provided. For educated readers, the style of the scriptures was a serious obstacle. Like later generations of classically trained theologians, they thought that the Greek of the New Testament, and the Latin of early translations, really was the 'language of fishermen' (Gamble 1995: 32–40). By comparison with the classical Greek prose that was the model for late antique rhetoric, the style of the New Testament writers seemed basic and even ungrammatical, especially when Hebrew idiom affected Greek and Latin translations.

Early Latin translations of the Greek scriptures also seemed like 'translationese'. Augustine remarked that they were often confusing or just wrong, because they were made by 'anyone who had a text and thought he knew some Greek' (*DDC* 2.36). Many people in North Africa, a Latin-speaking area, knew some Greek; the books Speratus brought to his trial (see above) may have been Greek, rather than the earliest evidence for Latin versions of the scriptures. By the time Augustine wrote *Christian Teaching*, at the end of the fourth century, Origen in the mid-third century, and Jerome in Augustine's own time, had done serious work on the Hebrew text of the Old Testament. Jerome, prompted by Bishop Damasus of Rome (ch. 6), had also started work on a new Latin translation, the version known since the Council of Trent (1546) as the Vulgate (Latin *vulgatus*, 'in common use'), in hopes of making scripture acceptable to classically educated readers. At the start of the fourth century, Lactantius, a teacher of rhetoric at the imperial court, acknowledged that the rough style of scripture, and the quality of its interpreters, would not convince an educated audience (*Div. Inst.* 5.1.15–21). Augustine too was not impressed when he first turned from Cicero to the Bible (*Conf.* 3.5.9). An example may help readers to sympathise with him, whether or not they are familiar with classical Latin:

And the Lord spoke to Moses, saying, 'Go in, and speak to Pharaoh king of Egypt, that he should send the sons of Israel from his land.' Moses replied in the presence of the Lord, 'See, the sons of Israel do not hear me, and how will Pharaoh hear, especially as I am uncircumcised in the lips?' (Exodus 6.10–12)

This is a literal translation of the Vulgate:

locutusque est Dominus ad Moysen, dicens: Ingredere, et loquere ad Pharaonem regem Aegypti, ut dimittat filios Israel de terra sua. Respondit Moyses coram Domino: Ecce filii Israel non audiunt me, et quomodo audiet Pharao, praesertim cum incircumcisus sum labiis?

Jerome cites an older version of the last phrase in his commentary on Galatians (5.6): *ego autem sum praeputium habens in labiis*, literally 'for I am having a foreskin on my lips'. This disconcerting image does make sense, to a reader who realises that circumcision is a metaphor for purity. But it is understandable that when Augustine, before his baptism, asked Ambrose which book of the Bible he should read, and Ambrose recommended Isaiah, Augustine very soon put the book aside until he had more practice in understanding the style (*Conf.* 9.5.13).

Augustine's comment on 'anyone who had a text and thought he knew some Greek' has been taken to mean that the first Latin translators had a low educational level, and that the 'old Latin' versions of the Bible are written in the Latin that was in common use. This, unfortunately, is known as 'vulgar Latin' (*vulgaris*, 'common'), as distinct from the classical Latin that was the basis of education. Latin-speaking schoolboys, in Augustine's time, studied the Latin classics, especially Terence, Sallust, Cicero and Virgil, and were trained to make speeches, and to write, in the style of four or five centuries earlier. It is this classicising Latin that survives in literary texts. The 'old Latin' versions of the Bible can be reconstructed from quotations, and linguists would be delighted if this was evidence for the Latin that was generally spoken. But more detailed research (Burton 2000) shows that the translations were made by people who had enough education to look for the right word. If their style seems awkward to classically trained readers, it is because they tried to be faithful to the Greek text of the New Testament and to the Greek translation of the Hebrew scriptures. This Greek translation is called the Septuagint, from Latin *septuaginta*, 'seventy', because of the splendid story that seventy (or seventy-two) translators, working separately on the Hebrew text, were divinely inspired to produce the same translation. So Biblical Latin sounded strange to the classically educated, but, as Augustine remarked, people who were brought up on Scripture thought that classical Latin sounded odd (*DDC* 2.14.21). There is no distinct 'Christian Latin', or Christian Greek, but Latin or Greek written by Christians is often marked by Bible quotations, rhythms and metaphors, and of course by technical theological terms.

ACCESS TO EDUCATION

We cannot assume either that many Christians lacked education or that Christians had higher levels of literacy than most. But there is still an argument that Christianity offered unusually wide access to education, because of its tradition, inherited from Judaism, of reading and commenting on scripture in regular meetings for worship (ch. 2). The closest analogy for this practice was not in Roman civic or elective cults, but in the use of philosophic texts to provide theology, ethical teaching, and advice on lifestyle. When the first-century Jewish writers Philo and Josephus attempted to explain Judaism to the Graeco-Roman world, they presented it as a range of philosophies (ch. 2), that is, ways of living in accordance with moral and religious beliefs, like Stoicism or Epicureanism.

Philosophy demanded time and attention, and some of the surviving texts are very difficult and technical. Platonist philosophy was especially influential in late antiquity; as in present-day epistemology and metaphysics, some late Platonist texts about questions of fundamental importance are preoccupied with debates among professionals that even other professionals find incomprehensible (Athanassiadi 1999, 2002). But philosophy was not confined to a highly educated elite. Some philosophers used all kinds of tactics to hold the attention of a wider audience: characterisation, dialogue, anecdote, direct address to the listener, satire on misguided ways of living. ('Diatribe' comes from Greek *diatribē*, a word used for a philosophic discourse.) The late first-century philosopher Epictetus, formerly slave of a slave of Nero, was particularly good at this lively teaching style (Long 2002). Many, perhaps most, philosophers lectured mainly to the sons of the elite, in the final stage of their higher education. But there might still be a very varied audience for their books, for many people called themselves *philosophos*, meaning not that they were philosophers, but that they loved wisdom (J. Barnes 2002).

Augustine retold (*CD* 9.4) a story, borrowed from the second-century scholar Aulus Gellius, of the Stoic in the shipwreck. The Stoic was pale and trembling, and a fellow-passenger mocked him for not living up to his principles. As a Stoic, he ought not to be afraid of death by drowning, because in Stoic teaching the only things that are really fearful are those that are really bad, and it is only wrong moral choices that are really bad.

When the danger passed, Gellius asked the Stoic to explain. Seeing that he was a serious enquirer, the Stoic pulled out a book and expounded the difference between immediate physical reactions, which are not within our control, and assessments of the situation, which are. This story is interesting both because the Stoic was carrying a book (other philosophers complained that Stoics were always pulling out somebody's *Introduction to Stoicism* and *Basic Definitions* and other tedious works), and because other people had a general awareness of Stoic teaching.

But, as Augustine also pointed out in *City of God* (2.6), if civic cult does not teach religion and morality, it is not much help to say that elective cults and philosophers do. Elective cults typically required initiation, and their teachings were confidential to the initiates: this is why they are commonly called 'mystery' cults, from Greek *mustērion*, something that must be kept silent. What, Augustine asked, is the point of keeping silent about morality? As for philosophy, where are the temples to Plato? Anyone could go to a temple and make an offering to the god, but to encounter Plato, whose teachings Augustine regarded as the highest achievement of Greek philosophy, it was necessary to find a text (or perhaps a translation) and a teacher. Lactantius commented that philosophy was not for women, slaves and the poor, whereas Christianity offered free wisdom (*Div. Inst.* 3.25, 3.26.10–11). Augustine pointed up the contrast:

Let it be said in what places these precepts of gods who teach were habitually read out and often heard by the people who worship them, in the same way that we point to churches built for that purpose, wherever the Christian religion spreads [. . .] a church is like a lecture-room for both sexes and all ages. (*City of God* 2.6; G. Clark 2001b)

Preaching was a long-established Christian tradition. It was called in Greek *homilia*, a conversational address (hence 'homily', which now means a moral exhortation); the Latin equivalent is *sermo* (hence 'sermon'), which also meant 'conversation' or anything in a conversational style, for instance a philosopher's lecture. In Augustine's time, the comparison between a church and a lecture-room was obvious, especially if the church building was a basilica (ch. 1). The reader read out the passages of Scripture chosen for the day, and the bishop, or his deputy, sat in his high-backed chair to address the congregation. The earliest known portrait of Augustine shows him seated in his chair, one hand resting on the codex of the scriptures, the other holding the scroll that was the symbol of an educated man (Lancel 2002: xv). Usually (then as now) the Scripture readings were the starting-point for the address, and the preacher explained difficult passages as well as drawing morals. By the fourth century, many bishops were well educated, and they used in their preaching the techniques they had learned as their literature teacher (*grammaticus*) took them through a text, or during their training in rhetoric and philosophy (Kaster 1988, Young 1997).

So Christianity did uniquely offer increased access to book-based education. Anyone who cared to come to church could learn ethics and theology from a sacred text that was carefully explained to the congregation. There is a high proportion of sermons in the immense range of early Christian texts, because the sermons of expert preachers were taken down in shorthand for circulation. The generation of the late fourth century, Ambrose and Augustine in Latin, Basil and John Chrysostom in Greek, is outstanding for brilliance and productivity. ('Chrysostom' means 'golden mouth'.) Texts were usually shared by reading aloud to a group, so even Christians who were not literate had further access to preaching. Caesarius of Arles makes this point, preaching in southern France in the early sixth century: there is no excuse for not following up the Bible references in a sermon, for those who cannot read can hire a reader or join a group (*Ser.* 6.2; Klingshirn 1994a: 183–4).

This optimistic account has been challenged, most forcefully in an influential article by Ramsay MacMullen (1989). He argues, especially from the sermons of John Chrysostom, that Christian preaching in the late fourth century is like other forms of rhetoric in that it assumes an elite urban audience, rich and educated. John Chrysostom preached in Antioch and then in Constantinople, both wealthy and important cities with many churches. But, MacMullen says, poor people might not be within reach of a church, if they lived in the country. They might not be allowed in, because their clothing and general appearance marked them out as poor; and if they were allowed in, the language and content of the preaching would be well above their heads. There are counter-arguments (G. Clark 2001b). Beggars clustered at the doors of churches, as they still do, so that they could appeal to people going in or out. It does not follow that they were excluded, and it would be against Christian principles to do so unless they were actually disruptive or an obvious danger to health. John Chrysostom says that Christians in embroidered silks stand at the altar next to Christians in rags (*Homilia* 11 in 1 Thessalonians 4); it might be rhetorical overstatement, but it might be true.

Could the congregation understand the preaching? Some of John Chrysostom's sermons, and some of Augustine's, are obviously designed for an elite audience that needs to be impressed by the quality of Christian preaching; some of Basil's sermons on famine are aimed at rich donors (ch. 6; Holman 2001). These high-profile sermons are the most likely to have been revised before they were circulated in written form. But some of the extant sermons are lightly revised, if at all. Sunday by Sunday, as the shorthand writers recorded, Chrysostom and Augustine worked through the readings for the day, making sure that everyone in the congregation was with them. Their tactics are familiar to any lecturer. They watch the expressions and the body-language of their audience for understanding or puzzlement or inattention, they repeat and reinforce important points, they use memorable illustrations and punchy phrases, they make connections with last week's sermon, they ask rhetorical questions such as 'Now why does it say . . .?' (Once Augustine's congregation shouted out the answer: evidently he had told that story last week.) Sometimes they offer sound-bite dismissals of classical culture, reassuring their hearers that Christians know better. Ambrose, a former imperial governor preaching in an imperial capital, is generally more formal in style, but when he takes a mixed-ability baptism class through the Creed, he uses just the same techniques. Augustine, advising a deacon at Carthage on how to handle such a class (*De Catechizandis Rudibus* 15), warns him that some members will be widely read (and he should tactfully discover what exactly they have read), some will have had a literary education, some will have read nothing.

Of course the standard of preaching varied. The sermons that survive come from the great preachers, or at least from preachers who had a local following, so that the shorthand writers had a market. Nobody copied the sermons that made Basil worry about what his country bishops were saying in Cappadocia (Rousseau 1994: 42), or that prompted Caesarius of Arles to recommend reading out sermons by the Fathers (Klingshirn 1994a: 229–30). Some preaching must have been mediocre or even misguided. But Christian leaders recognised their obligation to make the good news reach the poor and the country people and foreigners. In the mid-fourth century, the missionary bishop Ulfila devised an alphabet for the Gothic language so that he could translate the Bible for the Goths. (He left out the book of Kings, because the Goths were quite war-minded enough already.) Ulfila, according to fifth-century church historians, taught the Goths an Arian form of Christianity (ch. 2; Heather and Matthews 1991: 133–53). In the late fourth century, John Chrysostom ensured that Gothic troops in the imperial service had a church in Constantinople where catholic clergy took services in Gothic (Theodoret, *Historia Ecclesiastica* 5.30), and preached there himself, presumably with an interpreter. Augustine tried to find a Punic-speaking bishop for a rural district (*Ep.* 209.2). There is no evidence that anyone ever worried about the shortage of philosophers who spoke Gothic or Punic.

How many Christians could follow up preaching, as Caesarius urged, by reading the Bible for themselves? It is not the easiest of texts, but it might be easier for people who had often heard it read. Christians made copies of scripture for circulation even before monasteries organised production in writing-rooms (*scriptoria*; Gamble 1995: 121–32). But so far as the evidence goes, the only Christians who were expected to learn to read, if they could not already, were those who joined monastic communities and would spend much of the day meditating on Scripture. This requirement also applied to women. Augustine took it for granted that the members of a community could read (Lawless 1987). Caesarius, in the Rule he wrote for his sister's community, said that no one should enter unless she already knew letters or would learn them (Klingshirn 1994b). In general, women are thought to have had even lower literacy levels than men, because most women led domestic lives, and some men thought it not only pointless but actually risky for a woman to be literate. But it would have been difficult to claim that a woman was wasting her time, or was up to mischief, if she read her Bible. At a higher educational level, committed Christian women of the Roman aristocracy learned Hebrew and read commentaries (G. Clark 1993: 137).

RIVAL BOOKS

Churches provided all age groups with an education in scripture, but did not give parents an alternative to the Roman educational system (G. Clark 1994: 17–20). Children could learn to read and write without hearing unsuitable stories of pagan gods (Dionisotti 1982): for instance, a surviving school text from Tebtunis in Egypt reads 'Good handwriting begins with well formed letters and a straight line. Imitate me.' But the curriculum soon introduced Homer for Greek speakers and Virgil for Latin speakers, and educated people were expected to show their education by using the classical style and making graceful classical allusions. Christian attitudes varied (Kaster 1988; C. Harrison 2000: 46–78). The Christians who show most anxiety are those who were themselves most intensely affected by literature. Jerome and Augustine argued that children absorb the false values of their early education (Jer. *Ep.* 122, Aug. *Conf.* 1.16.26). Basil argued that it is possible to select the good from classical literature and leave the bad, but this *Advice to the Young* is not one of his most persuasive works; perhaps he was more concerned to justify his own experience (Rousseau 1994: 48–57; Van Dam 2002: 181–8).

The emperor Julian characteristically saw the other side of the coin: if Christians rejected the values of classical literature, they should not teach it. In a rescript early in his reign (*C. Th.* 13.3.5) he said that teachers should be outstanding in morality as well as eloquence. Some months later, he observed in a letter (*Ep.* 36) that, now there was freedom of religion, no one was obliged to teach what he did not believe. Teachers of classical texts should follow traditional religion; those who thought the ancient classics mistaken should teach Matthew and Luke in church. This letter was generally interpreted as forbidding Christians to teach, or even (Aug. *CD* 18.52) to be taught; the historian Ammianus, much as he admired Julian, deplored it (22.10.7). But Julian was more concerned to argue that the religion he called Hellenic did have sacred texts: the divinely inspired classics of literature and philosophy (Athanassiadi 1992). Admittedly, Plato had banned Homer and other poets from his ideal state on the grounds that they told lies about the gods, but there was a long tradition of interpreting Homer allegorically (Lamberton 1986), using techniques that Christians often found helpful in relation to Jewish scripture (Young 1997).

There was also a range of texts that Julian, like many other intellectuals, believed to contain the ancient wisdom of non-Greek cultures and to teach the same fundamental truths (Copenhaver 1992: xxiv–xxx). Among the most famous is the Hermetic Corpus, the body of texts ascribed to Hermes Trismegistus (Thrice-Greatest Hermes), the Greek equivalent of the Egyptian god Thoth (Fowden 1986). In their present, Greek, form they must belong to the early centuries CE, but the philosopher Iamblichus, whose works Julian greatly admired, thought that they had inspired Pythagoras and Plato. Another such text is the *Chaldaean Oracles* (Athanassiadi 1999), supposedly the wisdom of Babylon, compiled in Greek hexameters in the second century CE. Porphyry wrote a philosophical commentary on the *Oracles*. It is difficult now to understand, from the fragments, why he thought them so profound, but he was equally puzzled by what Christians saw in their texts, and denounced the use of allegory to make the Jewish scriptures more acceptable (G. Clark 1999b).

When they were not in polemical mode, philosophers sometimes added 'Hebrew wisdom' to the roll call of non-Greek cultures. The Jews had come from Egypt and settled near Phoenicia, and these were acknowledged to be two of the most ancient cultures; Hebrew could be counted as Assyrian. (Celsus argued that Christianity was divergent Judaism, which in turn was divergent Egyptian wisdom: Origen, *C. Cels.* 3.5.) Jews earned respect for keeping the laws of their long-ago legislator Moses, and their monotheism and their refusal to make images of God won approval from philosophers who engaged in critique of traditional religion (ch. 1). Jews and Christians could even argue that the best achievements of Greek philosophy came from

Judaism, for Plato had visited Egypt, so must have learned from Moses. The Platonist philosopher Numenius, who came from Apamea in Syria, called Plato 'Moses speaking Attic Greek', and Augustine said that Moses predated Hermes Trismegistus by four generations (*CD* 18.39). Christians too laid claim to an ancient tradition, on the grounds that Christianity was the fulfilment of Judaism and was foretold in the Jewish scriptures, and argued that Christianity was the best possible philosophy, both in its metaphysics and in its lifestyle. Some (ch. 1, ch. 6) saw Roman religion as demonic delusion, others saw it as aspiring to the understanding that Christianity had achieved.

So there was potential for incorporating Christianity, and Judaism, into the range of Roman or Hellenic religion, provided that Jewish and Christian theologies could be interpreted as 'soft monotheism' (ch. 1), that is, a belief in one god that allowed for lesser divine beings, and provided that their followers were willing to understand other beliefs as an approach to the same God. Almost two thousand years later, these questions are not resolved. Perhaps the best opportunity for dialogue came just before the outbreak of persecution, in the last years of the third century and the first years of the fourth (ch. 3; Digeser 2000). The anti-Christian Porphyry, according to Augustine (*CD* 19.23), was prepared to accept Jesus as one more great teacher, acknowledged by oracles, whose teachings had been distorted by Christians: as later ages put it, 'Jesus proclaimed God and the church proclaimed him.' The Christian Lactantius was prepared to engage with the great tradition of Roman law and Greek philosophy in an attempt to show that Christian teaching fulfilled, rather than rejecting, classical culture's search for justice and truth. But rhetoric and self-righteousness, or the political agenda of Diocletian, blocked out these attempts at dialogue.

Porphyry, again according to Augustine, said that he had not found a 'universal way' of salvation: not in philosophy, or in Indian practices, or in Chaldaean initiations (*CD* 10.30). Augustine contrasted this with the universal way offered by Christianity. Some hopeful modern scholars have thought that Porphyry (who in *On Abstinence* is an extreme intellectual snob) came to want a way of salvation that was accessible to all and that his letter to his wife Marcella approves the faithful observance of traditional cult, with deeper understanding for those who were capable. Iamblichus, his younger contemporary, offered this kind of understanding, defending (in the text that the Renaissance scholar Ficino called *The Mysteries of Egypt, Babylon and Assyria*) even animal sacrifice and processions of phallic symbols as appropriate offerings to the powers that govern the material universe. When Julian attempted to revive Hellenic religion, his problem was not the lack of sacred texts, but the lack of structure for religious education. His morally sound *grammatici* might have provided moral education, but how many parents could pay for it? He began the process (*Ep.* 89) of appointing priests for their moral qualities, and organising them into a hierarchy with rules of life and a commitment to care for humanity (*philanthrōpia*, which means general benevolence rather than active charity in the Christian sense, O'Meara 2003: 122). Perhaps these temple clergy could have offered simple instruction, with philosophers to provide advanced theology; perhaps the short treatise by Sallustius, *The Gods and the World* (Nock 1926) was intended as the basis for catechism; but it did not happen. Augustine used heavy irony against a correspondent: 'But, you will object, all those old stories about the life and morals of the gods are to be understood and interpreted quite differently by the wise. Why, only the other day we heard such improving interpretations read out to the people gathered in the temples!' (*Ep.* 91.5). Julian's plans were still a long way from the bishop in his chair with his codex of scripture, explaining it week by week to anyone who cared to come.

CHAPTER 6

Triumph, disaster or adaptation?

Never arrange a marriage. Never recommend anyone for public service. Never accept a dinner invitation in your home town.

(Advice from Ambrose, bishop of Milan, on being a bishop: Possidius, *Life of Augustine* 27)

Give me, emperor, the earth cleansed of heretics, and I will give you heaven in return. Help me eliminate heretics, and I will help you eliminate the Persians.

(Nestorius, newly appointed bishop of Constantinople 428–31, in a public address to Theodosius II: Socrates, *History of the Church* 7.29)

At the beginning of the fourth century Christians were experiencing the most sustained and intensive effort ever made to eliminate their religion (ch. 3). Ten years later Constantine and Licinius, then co-rulers of the Roman empire, declared freedom of religious belief and worship, and specifically ended the persecution of Christians. At the end of the fourth century, Theodosius I and his imperial colleagues declared to the Urban Prefect of Rome that anyone who engaged in animal sacrifice, visits to temples or veneration of images offended against divine and human law (*C. Th.* 16.10.10, 391 CE). The penalties remain vague unless the offender holds public office. Any official who enters a temple to worship, and any member of his staff who fails to report him, is liable to a heavy fine, on a sliding scale according to his status. A year later, an even more comprehensive law (*C. Th.* 16.10.12) addressed to the Praetorian Prefect banned sacrifice, private rites in honour of household deities, offering incense, garlanding trees and building turf altars. If an offender owned the property where this happened, he lost it; if not, he was liable for a heavy fine.

That was mild in comparison with a law that Christian emperors addressed a decade earlier (*C. Th.* 5.9, 382 CE) to the Praetorian Prefect of the East. It required the 'extreme penalty', that is, death, probably by burning, for Manichaeans, for other extreme ascetics, and, remarkably, for those who 'meet to celebrate Easter on a day that does not accord with religion'. In this context, that means the 'quartodecimans', literally 'four-teeners', who celebrated Easter at Passover, on the fourteenth day of the Jewish lunar month Nisan (Mitchell 1999). The Prefect was charged to search them out and to accept denunciations (contrast Trajan's instructions to Pliny on the treatment of Christians, ch. 2). Perhaps the 'wrong kind of Christian' seemed worse than the pagan who had not yet understood the truth; such Christians were also far fewer in number and lower in status than the pagans, and could be treated more harshly.

How did this transformation happen, in less than a century? There used to be an accepted narrative that went like this. In 312 Constantine won a victory that gave him access to Rome, and ascribed it to the support of the Christian god. He chose the Christian church as a support-base, perhaps because of his upbringing and his personal conviction, perhaps because it offered an empire-wide network of preachers and congregations. Nobody could have predicted an openly Christian emperor, but Constantine, and his son and successor Constantius II, so strengthened the position of the church that the traditional religion came to be seen as unacceptable. Paganism and heresy (ch. 2) were more clearly defined in opposition to orthodox Christianity, and came under increasing pressure. Julian the apostate, successor of Constantius, was the only post-Constantinian emperor to renounce Christianity, and his brief reign (361–3) showed that a pagan revival was no longer possible. The policies of subsequent emperors varied between severity and toleration, but by the end of the century Theodosius I, a secure and confident Christian emperor, was able to ban all manifestations of paganism. But there was (as always) a price to pay for official funding: a flood of insincere adherents, bishops chosen for their political contacts, emperors interfering in theology and church government, and a massive administrative load for church leaders.

Every stage of this narrative has been questioned. How much did Constantine understand about Christianity when he first declared his support, or at any later stage of his reign? Did he foresee that his support would have a wider effect than was usual when an emperor had a favourite cult, or was imperial intervention in theological debates as much an unintended consequence as the emergence of bishops as an alternative power? Did Julian fail to restore the traditional religion only because he did not live long, or because he was trying to impose his own brand of religion? What exactly was 'paganism' or 'heresy', what effect did legislation have, and what effect was it ever expected to have? Was there a Christian church, or was there rather an assortment of churches often in dispute, whose members were not easily distinguishable from the pagans and Jews of their communities? Did authentic Christianity survive the support of Constantine, or did Christianity adapt to become an acceptable official religion for Roman society?

IMPERIAL FAVOUR AND ITS EFFECTS

The question of Constantine and the church is another example of the problem of sources (ch. 2). The church historian Eusebius (ch. 1) is the major source for Constantine, to the point that they have to be studied together (T. Barnes 1981). He made a practice of citing official documents: in the years before Constantine, Christians had cited imperial rescripts to argue for toleration (ch. 3), and now they could cite them to argue for important benefits (Millar 1977: 577–90). Eusebius gave his readers a Greek translation of the document, inaccurately known as the 'Edict of Milan', that declared an end to the persecution of Christians (*EH* 10.5.2–14: Constantine and his co-ruler Licinius had agreed this policy at Milan, but what Eusebius translated was a letter from Licinius, who was based at Nicomedia on the Bosphorus, to the provincial governor). In citing other letters from Constantine, Eusebius showed how Constantine's initial involvement with the church could be interpreted. The letters have a specific context in the 'Donatist controversy', the claim by some North African Christians that others had betrayed the faith in time of persecution and could not validly baptize or ordain to church office (ch. 3). The Donatist dispute can be reconstructed because both sides had documents read into the minutes of councils; the Council of Carthage in 411, chaired by an imperial commissioner who was charged with stopping the violence, is especially well documented (Lancel 2002: 287–305). Eusebius, working in Palestine, knew little about Latin-speaking churches (Lawlor and Oulton 1927: 2.36–7), and may have had access only to the documents that created precedents for imperial intervention.

The 'Edict of Milan', following a precedent set by the emperor Gallienus after the persecution of the mid-third century (ch. 3), ordered that property owned by the Christian community should be returned to the owners; it further suggested official compensation for those who had acquired such property. Eusebius cited (10.5.15–17) a follow-up letter from Constantine to Anulinus, proconsul of Africa, with the tendentious heading (added by Eusebius or a later editor) 'Copy of another Imperial Ordinance indicating that the gift was made only to the Catholic Church'. 'Catholic' means 'universal', and it is not clear that Constantine had realised there were rival claimants to this status. He knew this by the time of the next letter cited by Eusebius (10.5.18–20): it is addressed to Miltiades bishop of Rome and refers to charges made against Caecilian bishop of Carthage by some of his colleagues. This, though Eusebius does not say so, was the moment when, according to Caecilian's supporters, his opponents brought in the imperial power to settle a church dispute. Again, there was a precedent (ch. 3): in the late third century, the emperor Aurelian settled the disputed owner-ship of church buildings in Antioch by asking the bishops of Rome and Italy which claimant they recognised as the rightful bishop (7.30.19–21). Constantine duly summoned Caecilian to have his case heard by Bishop Miltiades, and went further in an attempt to resolve disputes. Eusebius also cited (10.5.21–4) his letter summoning Chrestus bishop of Syracuse to a council of 'very many bishops from innumerable places': they were to meet at Arles to settle all disputes, and Chrestus was authorised to ask his local governor for transport. These two letters set a precedent for imperial inter-vention in church disputes, with appropriate resources. Later in the fourth century, the historian Ammianus complained (21.16.18) that the impe-rial transport system was overloaded with bishops travelling at the public expense.

The next two letters show Constantine the benefactor of the church. Caecilian (*EH* 10.6) is authorised to collect from the finance minister a large sum for the expenses of named clergy, and told to ask the proconsul for help if he continues to have trouble from 'certain persons of unstable mind'; and the proconsul Anulinus (10.7) is told that clergy in the 'Catholic Church over which Caecilian presides' are to be exempted from public office. This was a major financial benefit, for members of local councils (*decuriones*) paid the bills and made up shortfalls in tax collections. Exemptions were a well established reward for individuals, such as doctors or teachers (Kaster 1988), who made an important contribution to their community, or who were high-ranking public servants. But the global exemption for Caecilian's clergy was generalised for the entire empire, and soon had to be restricted, both because local councils complained about losing recruits and because some people joined the clergy for financial reasons (Brown 2002: 29–30).

Eusebius then returned to the wrongdoing of Constantine's colleague Licinius, and did not discuss the immediate or the longer-term problems that resulted from these familiar signs of imperial favour. The feud in North Africa might have been just as bitter even if Constantine's gifts had not put money and property and status at stake, for serious theological differences were reinforced by group loyalties and memories of betrayal (ch. 5, ch. 3; C. Harrison 2000: 145–52). Schism (Greek *schisma*, 'division' or 'tear' as in a torn fabric) is a division caused by refusal to be in communion with other Christians, and such refusals always result from theological disagreement. The Donatists believed that the church cannot include those who have betrayed the faith: Augustine said that they saw the church as Noah's Ark, containing only clean creatures and walled against the ocean. He preferred the image of the net (Matthew 13.47–50) that catches good and bad fish, and in *City of God* he developed his account of the church that includes both citizens of the city of this world, who are motivated by the rewards it offers, and citizens of the city of God, who are motivated by the love of God. Only God knows who is which.

The Donatist claim to be the true catholic church was weakened because the dispute was local. Augustine declaimed 'Throughout the world Heaven's thunder rolls, announcing that God's house is being built; and the frogs sit in their marsh and croak "We're the only Christians!"' (*Enarrationes in Psalmos* 95.11). But Constantine's involvement in this local dispute had empire-wide effects: joining the Christian clergy became an attractive career path, offering exemption from public service, control of extensive property, and high status in the community. Bishops earned their exemption, not just by the religious observance that Constantine gave as a reason, but because he greatly increased their workload as arbitrators. In the mid-first century, Paul told Christians to take their disputes to the bishop rather than to a Roman judge (1 Corinthians 6.1–8): Constantine wanted bishops to deal with any case in civil law where the parties accepted their jurisdiction (Harries 1999: 191–211; Garnsey and Humfress 2001: 74–80). His policy was so surprising that a senior official, Ablabius, wrote asking for clarification. Constantine's response (preserved separately from the laws collected in the Theodosian Code: Lee 2000: 218) affirmed that a case must be referred to the bishop if either party requested it. There could be no appeal from the bishop's judgement; and if the bishop agreed to testify for one party in a case, no other evidence was to be heard. This policy also ensured, as Augustine remarked to his congregation, that there was always someone who was angry with the bishop, and who would accuse him of taking bribes or seeking favour (*En. Ps.* 25.13). Constantine may have adopted this policy because the backlog of court cases and appeals was an urgent problem; if so, intervention in church disputes may have been the price that he had to pay (Drake 2000). It is also possible that even more cases had to be heard, if people who would have avoided the expense and endemic bribery of the courts were prepared to go to a bishop.

Constantine showed great respect for the judgement of bishops in legal cases, but he also took it for granted that he could and should intervene in church concerns; that he could summon bishops, especially when he had authorised their transport, and send them home again (Optatus, *Appendix* 5); and that failure to comply with the emperor's summons was punishable (Eusebius, *Vita Constantini* 4.42). People who disliked the results of his interventions questioned the right of an emperor to judge bishops and theological problems. In the mid 350s the senior bishop Hosius (Ossius) of Cordoba, who had advised Constantine on church matters, used one of Jesus' most famous sayings to challenge the intervention of Constantine's son and successor Constantius II in favour of Arian theology (ch. 2, and below). Jesus was faced with the question whether Jews should pay taxes to the Roman empire. If he said yes, he was a collaborator; if he said no, he was a rebel.

They sent some Pharisees and some of Herod's people to trap him. They came and said, 'Teacher, we know that you are sincere and afraid of no one: you are not concerned with a man's status, but teach God's way in truth. Is it permitted to pay tax to Caesar or not? Should we pay it or not?' He saw through their pretence and said, 'Why do you test me? Bring me a denarius and let me see it.' They brought it, and he said, 'Whose image and inscription is this?' They said, 'Caesar's'. Jesus said to them, 'Pay Caesar what is Caesar's, and God what is God's.' (Mark 12.13–17)

The traditional English translation 'render unto Caesar' is still in use to mean 'give the authorities their due'. In a letter cited by the anti-Arian Athanasius (*Historia Arianorum* 44), Hosius used Jesus' reply to make a clear distinction between what belongs to the emperor and what belongs to God: 'God has put the kingdom in your hands: he has entrusted the concerns of the church to us.' That is, the church, its property and its teaching belong to God and God's ministers, not to the emperor.

Church concerns dominate the sources for Constantine's reign, but they are likely to have been low on his agenda unless there was a threat to public order. A decade after he summoned the council of Arles (314), a theological dispute in the church of Alexandria led to his most famous intervention, the Council of Nicaea (325). He was at last in control of the eastern Mediterranean, and may have been genuinely shocked by the disagreements he found among Christians; moreover, Alexandria had a tradition of rioting which might disrupt the vital shipments of Egyptian grain from the Alexandria docks. Eusebius, in his *Life of Constantine* (*VC* 2.63–72), cites an impassioned letter of Constantine urging peace and forbearance, for the dispute is not about some new heresy, but about 'small and very insignificant questions'. This seems like an astonishing display of ignorance, for the dispute was about the theology of Arius, and on one inter- pretation of what Arius taught, Jesus Christ was not God incarnate but a created being, and therefore did not unite God and humanity. But, if Arius has been misunderstood (R. Williams 2001), Constantine had a point: Arius and his bishop agreed on fundamentals and differed in emphasis. The dispute spread, and in 325 Constantine had a church synod (Greek *sunodos*, 'meeting') transferred from Ancyra, an inland city of Asia Minor, to Nicaea on the north-western coast. It was, he said, more convenient for bishops from Italy and Europe, and the climate was very pleasant. It was also conveniently near his court at Nicomedia.

Constantine said that 'about three hundred' bishops attended; the list of signatures shows that this is an overestimate. (Tradition raised the atten- dance to three hundred and eighteen, the same number as the servants of Abraham in Genesis 14.14.) Eusebius described (*VC* 3.10) how the Council met in one of the great rooms of the palace. Constantine had advisers, not soldiers, as his escort; he wore his imperial robes, but he waited for the bishops' assent before he sat on his golden chair. The palace blazed with light as the bishops went to dine with the emperor, fearlessly passing the drawn swords of his bodyguard. It must have been an extraordinary expe- rience for Eusebius, whose teacher Pamphilus had died a martyr and who had himself lived through persecution (ch. 3). But the emperor's deference to spiritual authority did not mean that the council could end without an agreed statement, and it was the emperor who suggested (presumably after prior consultation) the key word that expressed the relationship of Christ to God. This was *homoousios*, 'of the same essential being' (ch. 2), a technical term of Greek philosophy that does not occur in the Bible. Eusebius, for one, had great difficulty explaining to his congregation why he had signed both the agreed statement of belief and the accompanying denunciations of unacceptable beliefs, the anathemas (ch. 5). Two bishops who were willing to sign the statement of belief did not sign the anathemas because they thought Arius had been misrepresented: both were exiled.

This was an ominous precedent. Athanasius, bishop of Alexandria from 328 and a strong supporter of Nicene theology, was exiled five times as imperial policy and church politics changed (Drake 2000). In 385 Priscillian bishop of Avila was tried by a secular court, and the pious emperor Gratian confirmed the sentence of execution. This looks like an even more ominous precedent for the late medieval Inquisition, which identified heretics then handed them over to the 'secular arm' for punishment. It is not a clear precedent, for Priscillian was convicted of practising magic, which was closely associated with treason against the emperor (Garnsey and Humfress 2001: 161). But many laws from the fourth and early fifth centuries (collected in *C. Th.* 16.5: Magnou-Nortier 2002) did treat heretics as offenders against the law. Heretics were excluded from privileges and forbidden to assemble or teach; they were deprived of their property or expelled from cities. In the final years of the fourth century, Jovinian, who wrote against extreme asceticism (ch. 4), was deported from Rome to an Adriatic island (*C. Th.* 16.5.53); in 412, heavy fines were imposed on Donatists (16.5.2). Such laws were probably a response to immediate protests or demands from Christian clergy, rather than a series of imperial initiatives against heresy. But the clergy not currently in favour might have agreed with Hosius that Caesar was interfering in God's concerns.

CHURCH AND STATE

The emperor had a duty to maintain the peace so that God could be worshipped, but did he have the authority to impose creeds and to judge priests and bishops? When non-Christian emperors ruled, Christians were taught to obey Roman law unless it conflicted with the worship of God (ch. 3). Paul wrote to Christians at Rome:

Let every soul be subject to the authorities that are in power. For there is no authority that is not subject to God, and the existing authorities [the older English translation is 'the powers that be'] are appointed by God. So a man who opposes authority opposes God's arrangement, and those who oppose will bring judgement on themselves. Officials inspire fear not in those who behave well, but in those who behave badly. You want not to fear authority? Act well, and authority will approve of you, for it is God's servant for your good. If you act badly, be afraid: authority does not carry a sword for nothing. (Romans 13.1–4)

Paul accepted the authority of Roman government to maintain law and order, if necessary by the 'right of the sword', that is, the right of a governor to order execution. (Four centuries later, 'if you want not to fear authority, act well' was set in the mosaic floor of the tax office at Caesarea Maritima in Palestine: Brown 2002: 86.) How, then, did the authority of a Christian emperor relate to the authority of a Christian bishop? The tradition of imperial panegyric gave the emperor a special status in relation to God, and Eusebius follows this tradition in his *Life of Constantine* (*VC* 4–6; Cameron and Hall 1999: 187). Constantine, according to Eusebius, once told a group of bishops that he was a bishop (*episkopos*, literally 'supervisor') for those outside the church (*VC* 4.24). He wanted to be buried among the apostles, and in his mausoleum, his sarcophagus was surrounded by twelve tombs or grave-markers for the twelve apostles (*VC* 4.60). This might be an outrageous claim to spiritual status, as bishop, or apostle, or even (on one interpretation of Eusebius' rhetoric) as the incarnate word of God. Alternatively, it might be an affirmation of Constantine's Christian commitment.

Constantine's understanding of his relationship to the God of the Christians may have been similar to his predecessor Diocletian's understanding of his relationship to Jupiter. Jupiter, the supreme god, gave Diocletian victory and authorised his rule (Digeser 2000: 27–30); he and his junior colleague Maximian had the titles Jovius (belonging to Jupiter) and Herculius (belonging to Hercules, the deified son of Jupiter). In return, Diocletian was bound to ensure that Jupiter was worshipped throughout his empire, and that there was no obstacle to communication from the gods through sacrifices and oracles; that may explain (ch. 3) his attempt to eliminate Christians, who refused to worship the gods and obstructed communication from the gods. Constantine similarly ascribed his victory to the God of the Christians, and believed that he had a special relationship with that God, which entailed responsibility for the worship of that God. But he did not persecute worshippers of other gods: he had seen persecution fail (Drake 2000). He was increasingly outspoken in his personal support for Christianity and in his dismissal of traditional religion, but he made it possible for non-Christians in his army and his court to worship 'the supreme divinity', the divine power, often symbolised by the sun, that had many names (Lane Fox 1986: 615; Edwards 2003: xi–xii). He was baptised only when he knew he was dying, but that does not show he was previously uncommitted. Many Christians believed that baptism cleansed sin, but that post-baptismal sin could not be cleansed. Sin goes with the territory of being emperor; Constantine symbolically replaced his purple imperial robe with the white robe of baptism. Julian, gleefully followed by anti-Christian authors, declared that Constantine had to be Christian, for his crimes included the murder of his wife and son, and nobody else would have him (*Caesars* 336b; Lieu and Montserrat 1996: 16–18).

Constantine demonstrated his support for Christianity, in the same way that previous emperors had shown support for their favourite cults, by making lavish gifts. The 'Book of the Pontiffs' (*Liber Pontificalis*, Davis 1989) records gifts made to the church of Rome under each of its bishops. (They are called *pontifex*, 'pontiff', because they took over the title of the major Roman priesthood.) Until Constantine, these gifts are modest. In

Constantine's reign there are long lists of spectacular gifts: land, church buildings, marble, gold and silver church fittings, light-fittings and endowments for lamp oil. Lights were especially important for churches, because Christian worship took place inside buildings (ch. 1), whereas traditional temples had their altars outside. Light from windows and lamps, reflected from mosaic and precious metals, was a powerful symbol of the light of God illuminating the world. Medieval Christians improved on Constantine's gifts with the 'donation of Constantine' (Edwards 2003), a document (proved to be inauthentic by the fifteenth-century humanist Lorenzo Valla) that formally recognised the separate powers of church and state. Constantine did not do that, but his personal gifts to churches and clergy, his recognition that the church could legally inherit wealth from donors (*C. Th.* 16.2.4), and the role he gave bishops in jurisdiction, ensured that bishops could be very important people in their community.

Some churches reacted to this new role by choosing as their bishops men who already had status and contacts, rather than those who had spiritual authority. Even in 325, the Council of Nicaea noted in its second canon (Greek *kanōn*, 'rule') that some people had been baptised and simultaneously made priest or bishop after only a brief period of instruction, and that this must stop. The rule had a limited effect. 'Canon law', a systematic collection of rulings on church discipline, probably began when the emperor Justinian decided, in 545, that the canons of four great councils, including Nicaea, had the status of law (see Hess 2002 for earlier developments). In the early centuries, the canons of one council might be inconsistent, deliberately or from lack of knowledge, with those of another council; they might be unknown to anyone who had not attended the council; and they might simply be disregarded. (Roman law presented comparable problems: Garnsey and Humfress 2001: 58–64.) Augustine, for instance, was assured that there were precedents for his consecration as bishop of Hippo while the previous bishop was still alive: he found out later that a canon of Nicaea forbade this (Lancel 2002: 183). Ambrose of Milan, a strong supporter of Nicene theology, became bishop in contravention of the second Nicene canon: he was baptised, ordained to successive orders of ministry, and consecrated, all with great speed, after many years as imperial governor of the region. According to his biographer Paulinus (*Vita Ambrosii* 9), he tried to show that a governor was not a suitable candidate: he used, for the first time, his power to have suspects tortured for information, and caused prostitutes to visit his house (Paulinus does not explain why: perhaps to give evidence?). A more political interpretation (McLynn 1994: 44–52) makes Ambrose a compromise candidate, skilfully contriving a show of unanimity in a violent dispute between Nicenes and Arians. If so, unanimity, however contrived, was preferable to the election of Damasus as bishop of Rome in 366, with a body count of 137 or more in the struggle for a basilica (Ammianus Marcellinus 27.3.13; Hunt 1998: 267).

Ambrose, an experienced and well-connected politician, was able to insist on the distinction between the concerns of Caesar and the concerns of God. We have only his account of three famous confrontations with the imperial family, written in letters to his sister (head of an ascetic community of women) in the awareness that such letters would be widely circulated. In 385 Ambrose resisted an attempt by the young emperor Valentinian (and his mother) to assign a basilica to Arian clergy, arguing (*Ep.* 76[20]) that the emperor had no power over the things that are God's. At one stage of the dispute soldiers surrounded the church, but some of them joined in the service; at another, members of Ambrose's congregation, including Augustine's mother Monica, occupied the church, and Ambrose introduced the eastern practice of congregational hymn-singing to keep up morale (Aug. *Conf.* 9.7.15). In 388 the bishop of Callinicum, on the Euphrates, encouraged monks to burn a synagogue. Jewish religion had legal protection (ch. 1), and the emperor Theodosius quite properly required the bishop to pay for rebuilding the synagogue; but Ambrose preached a sermon that Theodosius recognised as a rebuke, and Theodosius backed down. The most famous confrontation of Ambrose and Theodosius (*Ep.* 51[20]) was quickly presented as an image of the church's spiritual authority even over the emperor. In 390 an imperial commander at Thessaloniki imprisoned a popular charioteer (the modern equivalent would be a footballer) for immoral conduct. The commander was killed in the riot that followed; Theodosius ordered the troops to deal with this disrespect, but they over-reacted and killed innocent people. Fifth-century church historians said that Ambrose excluded the emperor from communion and required him to do penance (Thdt. *HE* 5.18). A more political interpretation (McLynn 1994: 315–30) sees a 'repentance opportunity' that demonstrated the piety of Theodosius and defused the situation (surely an idea whose time has returned?). But there would be no such opportunity without acknowledgement that bishops have, in principle, moral authority over heads of state.

OPTING OUT

Ambrose and Augustine were outstanding bishops, but both struggled to find time for prayer and Bible study (Aug. *Conf.* 6.3.3; *De Opere Monachorum* 37). It could be argued either that they should not have been burdened by their impossible workload of management and arbitration, or that their skill in rhetoric and administration should have been used in the service of the empire. When Paulinus of Nola (ch. 4) gave up his social and political status to lead an ascetic life at the shrine of St Felix, his friend Ausonius wrote him reproachful and puzzled poems (Trout 1999: 68–77; Conybeare 2000:147–57). Of the great fourth-century generation of preachers, Basil and Jerome and John Chrystostom were well qualified for public service careers, Ambrose had a successful public career and Augustine had hoped for one. Did Constantine's support for the Christian church drain talent from Roman imperial administration? Did Christianity, as Gibbon (ch. 1) argued, undermine the values of the Roman empire, both because it diverted resources and abilities away from public service, and because Christian pacifism was incompatible with defence against crime and aggression? Even in the second century, Celsus (Origen, *C. Cels.* 8.75) accused Christians of avoiding public responsibilities; Origen replied, a century later, that service in the church was more important to the general welfare.

Constantine's reason for exempting clergy from council duties was the importance of religious observance, and he ensured that bishops contributed to society (above). But there were Christians who sought to escape such commitments, and Christian asceticism (ch. 4) took to extremes the Roman philosophical tradition of simplicity and detachment from worldly concerns. Philosophical detachment was compatible with sustaining family and civic commitments, whereas (some) Christian preachers argued that virginity was better than having children, and that surplus wealth should be given in charity, not preserved for the family or used in civic benefaction (see below). Roman tradition admired devoted and unselfish service to the state: its heroes were such men as Regulus, who died by torture rather than break his oath or disadvantage Rome; Cincinnatus, who returned from peasant farming to save Rome; great generals and emperors who extended the empire and preserved the peace; even a few women whose chastity, piety and loyalty contributed to the good of Rome. Christians were urged to take as their heroes, in succession to the martyrs, ascetic men and women who abandoned their families and their cities to live in poverty and isolation.

Augustine, retelling the story of the imperial civil servants who came upon the *Life of Antony* (ch. 4), makes them see a choice. They could go on working to be 'friends of the emperor', that is, trusted imperial advisers, with all the risks of a political career; or they could be friends of God at once, just by making a decision. This choice is not distinctively Christian, for some traditions of philosophy, especially Epicureanism and some versions of Platonism, also urged a retreat from family and civic duties. Christian preachers (ch. 5) presented this 'ascetic mentality' to a wider range of people, but how many Christians ever decided for the ascetic life, or even felt that they ought to consider it? The insistent preaching of Basil and John Chrysostom and Augustine does not suggest a rush to the monasteries. Only a few people are known to have moved from public service to church service; and church service increasingly became public service, especially in dealing with legal disputes and in providing for the poor. Even Paulinus, the classic example of renouncing the world, behaved in his ascetic retreat at Nola much like a Roman nobleman on his estate, and was a most effective networker with other ascetic Christians (Trout 1999).

Augustine had to engage with the second charge, that Christian teaching is incompatible with protection against crime and aggression, both because non-Christians used the argument and because some Christians asked whether they should continue in military or civil service (Atkins and Dodaro 2001). Romans liked to believe that they fought 'just wars', that is, wars in which the Romans were not the aggressors, but resisted attack or defended their allies. Cicero included in a philosophical dialogue the comment that in defending their allies the Romans have conquered the whole world (Cicero, *De Republica* 3 fr. 2), but as this comment survives only because a grammarian quoted it, we cannot tell whether Cicero intended his speaker to convey irony. Christians similarly rejected aggression, but they had, and still have, divergent views on the use of war and punishment to restore or maintain peace. The Ten Commandments, accepted by Jews and Christians, include 'You shall not kill.' For some Christians, this is a total ban on taking human life: they point out that Jesus told his followers not to return violence for violence, but to 'turn the other cheek' when hit in the face (Matthew 5.38–9). For others, the commandment means 'You shall not murder': they make a distinction between lawful and unlawful killing, and think that it is permissible to kill if there is no other way to defend oneself or others. They point to episodes and passages in the New Testament that acknowledge the use of force (Helgeland–Daly–Burns 1985: 10–20).

So, when non-Christians ruled the empire, some Christians did not see a conflict between their religion and military service. A few soldiers made the choice to declare themselves Christian and take the consequences (ch. 3), but in the centuries before Constantine, Christians were not likely to be faced with a decision whether to order the taking of life. A Christian who reached a prominent position that carried the 'right of the sword', in the army or as a civil governor, would risk accusation if the public mood or the emperor's policy changed; he would also be expected to play his part in traditional religious ceremonies. From Constantine's reign on, a committed Christian might be in charge of troops or of law enforcement. If he ordered the taking of life, could he still share in communion (ch. 1)? Ambrose's advice (*Ep.* 50[25]) to a troubled Christian governor was that Studius might himself feel the need to abstain from communion after he had ordered an execution, but Ambrose could not require it. Studius had the authority of Paul (above): he was God's avenger against those who do evil.

Augustine, who agreed that 'You shall not kill' means 'You shall not murder', developed the account of 'just war' that is still in use (Markus 1983). For him, it is not the use of force that matters, but the motive for using it. A soldier is morally in the clear if he kills, either in war or as an executioner, not in anger or in the desire for vengeance, but for the sake of peace and on the orders of the proper authority. The person who has that authority is morally in the clear if he is motivated not by anger or hatred but by the need to preserve the peace, and if he uses no more violence than is necessary for that purpose. This widely accepted doctrine made it possible, in later centuries, for Christian clergy to bless whatever weapons were in use, but there have always been Christian voices of protest. Ambrose told Studius that many pagans took pride in having shed no blood during their term as governor. A contemporary of Augustine, possibly the British theologian Pelagius, wrote bitterly of the Christian judge who, at the end of a day ordering torture and execution, lolls on his cushions and complains to his friends about the contradictions of his job (*De Divitiis* 6, *PL* suppl. 1.1386).

NO CHANGE?

'What difference did Christianity make?' Ramsay MacMullen (1986) asked this fundamental question, and answered, in effect, 'Not a lot.' Constantine did not transform the Roman empire into a Christian society. War and crime continued. Slavery was not abolished, and slaves were not encouraged to seek any freedom other than spiritual freedom (Garnsey 1996): the cross appears on a 'return to owner' slave collar (*Inscriptiones Latinae Selectae* 8730). Family law in general maintained the moral standards of Roman tradition rather than those of Christian aspiration (Evans Grubbs 1995, Arjava 1996). Late antique legislation is notorious for cruel and unusual punishments, and they are especially prominent in the Theodosian Code, the collection of law made in the mid-fifth century on the orders of the devoutly Christian Theodosius II.

But there is also a question 'what difference would you expect?' Christian
ethics were close to the ethics of decent Romans (an argument used in Christian apologetic), and Roman law allowed behaviour that decent people
would avoid, whether or not they were Christian. Law has to be enforce-
able, and Christian emperors had to legislate for an empire that was not
consistently Christian. For instance, Roman law allowed divorce: Christians were taught to concede divorce to a non-Christian partner, but not
to seek divorce or to think themselves free to remarry, and the divorce
legislation of Christian emperors did not correspond to Christian principle (Arjava 1996). Roman law allowed fathers to decide against rearing a
newly born child, and to make that decision clear by *expositio,* 'putting out'
the baby: Christian emperors expressed disapproval, but did not forbid the
practice (G. Clark 1993: 48–9). Roman law tolerated extra-marital affairs for
men, provided that the woman concerned was not married or marriage-
able. When Constantine legislated (*Codex Justinianus* 5.26.1) that a man
cannot have a wife and a concubine at the same time, he was not trying
to impose Christian sexual morality on a resistant empire, but reaffirming
a legal principle (Evans Grubbs 1995). A concubine was by definition the
acknowledged partner of a man, so her children had a claim to inherit from
him; but a wife was by definition the woman whose children were the man's
legitimate heirs.

Similarly, when Constantine removed the legal disadvantages of the
unmarried and childless (*C. Th.* 8.16.1), he was not showing support for
Christian asceticism. Augustus imposed these disadvantages three centuries
earlier, probably as an incentive for producing children and as a disincen-
tive for legacy-hunters. They prevented unmarried and childless people
from inheriting, except from kin within the sixth degree of relationship.
In Roman law, the degree of relationship depends on how many 'acts of
generation' are required to create the relationship. Father and son are kin
in the first degree, brother and sister in the second, so the sixth degree
of kinship includes most of the people from whom a family inheritance
could reasonably be expected. Even so, the Augustan rule was resented,
and Constantine's reform could be dramatically presented as liberation
(Evans Grubbs 1995): but Christian ascetics ought not to have been interested in legacies anyway. Julian claimed that Constantine had disrupted
traditional laws and morality, but this seems to have been a characteristic
overstatement.

One difference that Christianity did make was in provision for the poor
(ch. 2; Garnsey and Humfress 2001: 107–31), both in practical terms and
in terms of ethics. There is a clear contrast between Christian preaching

on charitable giving and Roman ethical teaching on meeting one's obligations. 'Charity' comes from Latin *caritas*, 'dearness' or 'love', but Cicero
discusses gift-giving in the context of duties (Cicero, *On Duties*, late first
century BCE; Griffin and Atkins 1991), and Seneca in the context of confer-
ring and returning benefits (Seneca, *On Benefits*, mid-first century; Griffin
2003). They carefully assess the priorities and the requirements of obligation to family, friends, benefactors, and dependants. Philosophers taught
that everyone should recognise common humanity, but Romans did not
think they had an obligation to give to the poor just because the poor are
in need. Roman society expected the rich to engage in 'good works', large-
scale benefactions to which Paul Veyne gave the name 'euergetism' (from
Greek *euergetēs*, 'benefactor': Veyne 1976), but these 'good works' only inci-
dentally benefited the very poor. In a society without welfare provision, the
rich had to consider carefully who had legitimate claims on their support.
A benefactor's contributions to the city's tax bill relieved pressure on the
more prosperous citizens. His (or her, ch. 2) grand civic buildings provided
employment for labourers, but only until the building work was finished;
thereafter arches and porticoes might provide shelter for the homeless, but
benefactors were not praised for this. Cut-price sale of grain when the har-
vest was bad, and handouts of food or cash at festivals, may have reached
the very poor, provided that they could at least claim citizenship. At Rome,
tokens for subsidised grain or bread were not allocated by need, but were
hereditary or went with the house.

When Ambrose wrote his own *On Duties* in the late fourth century,
he offered advice as Cicero did on how to assess obligations, but for him,
charitable giving is a priority, and the question is what limits the clergy
may set to their giving (Davidson 2001). Lactantius (*Div. Inst.* 6.4.1) notes
the contrast between Christian valuation of the poor and lowly and the
attitude of Cicero (*Tusculan Disputations* 5.29), for whom poverty and lowliness begin a long list of apparent evils that the wise man may endure.
The poor are scarcely visible in Roman classical texts, unless they are
the respectable poor (Greek *penētes*), sturdy peasant farmers or artisans
and traders who work hard for a living, or people who are poor (Latin
pauper) in the sense that they cannot take on the duties of prominent citizens. Epictetus, the first-century philosopher who had once been a slave,
notices the destitute, but uses them as living proof that people who want
to be philosophers could survive with far fewer possessions. The reason for
philosophers to simplify their lifestyle is to liberate the soul from distractions
(ch. 4), not to achieve a surplus for distribution to the poor. The destitute
(Greek *ptōchoi*) come into focus in Christian texts, where charitable giving

becomes a primary obligation. Clement of Alexandria, in the second century, preached '*Who is the rich man who is saved?*' about the Gospel story that later inspired Antony to sell all his possessions (ch. 4). Clement saw no point in the rich making themselves destitute too, but he did argue that they would benefit from giving generously to the poor. Giving alms (the word comes from Greek *eleēmosunē*, 'showing pity') compensates for sin, and the recipient can return the gift by spiritual advice, or by praying for the giver.

Clement also suggested that the most effective form of charity was not impulse giving, but regular donation to the church's welfare fund. This tradition went back to the Jewish beginnings of Christianity (ch. 2). In the Acts of the Apostles, the role of the deacon (*diakonos*) is to administer this fund, and Paul's letters regularly ask for donations to help other Christian communities. Justin Martyr in the second century (*Apol.* 1, 67) and Tertullian in the early third century (*Apol.* 39), include regular voluntary donations among the Christian practices they hold up for praise. There were also special collections in emergencies, such as Cyprian's for the ransom of Christian prisoners (*Ep.* 62–3, mid-third century). In 251, according to Eusebius (*EH* 6.43.11) the church in Rome supported fifteen hundred widows and destitute people.

Welfare provision on this scale looks, to some historians, like another form of patronage, allowing the bishop to rival the traditional civic benefactors and build up his own support-base (Countryman 1980; Brown 2002). The distinction between traditional euergetism and Christian charity has been challenged, on the grounds that the activity of Roman officials and benefactors might extend to the very poor, whereas Christian bishops and donors might acquire an actual or symbolic retinue that had considerable political impact. There is a dramatic presentation of such a retinue in a poem by Prudentius (*Peristephanon* 2, late fourth century) on St Lawrence, deacon and martyr of the Roman church. When the prefect of the city demanded that Lawrence hand over the church's treasure, he asked for time, and assembled all the destitute and ailing poor who depended on the church. Such people were not an obvious support-base, but if they followed the traditional practice of escorting and applauding their benefactor, they demonstrated that he was doing his job; and perhaps their presence on the bishop's welfare-list (the *matricula*) gave them a kind of civic identity.

A famous example from late fourth-century Cappadocia shows the potential for rivalry in benefaction. Basil, soon to be bishop of Caesarea, came from a family with traditions of local patronage (Rousseau 1994, Van

Dam 2002). He wrote (*Ep.* 94) to the governor of Cappadocia, expressing surprise that the governor was not pleased by Basil's plans for a hospice and associated buildings outside the city. Hospices, one of the great welfare developments of the Christian empire, were not designed as hospitals to centralise medical care and training (Nutton 1986). Their purpose was to provide whatever care was needed for those who lacked family support, for example, babies 'put out' by families who could not raise them, and the destitute who were too ill or too old to work. Caesarea was at a junction of major roads, and Basil wanted to provide for those who travelled along them: a place to stay, with medical personnel, supplies of food and clothing, and a local market. By the early fifth century (Socrates, *Historia Ecclesiastica* 6.34.9) this complex was known as the 'Basileias', which might be a reference to the Kingdom (Greek *basileia*) of God; but it took its name from Basil.

The 'rival patronage' interpretation of charity differs from the 'sexual neurosis' interpretation of asceticism (ch. 4) in that it does not say 'We know better than you did what you were really doing', but 'We know what you were really doing and would not admit.' When Ambrose of Milan broke up church silver to ransom prisoners, he said (*De Officiis* 2.136–41) that he was obeying the teachings of Jesus. His opponents said he was really asserting his episcopal power over the donors whose names were engraved on their gifts, and this interpretation appeals to historians who think that religion is the pursuit of politics by other means. Some forms of conspicuous Christian giving seem to be directly in the tradition of benefaction that advertised a family. For example, Galla Placidia, daughter of Theodosius I, built a church at Ravenna, some time after 425, as an offering in thanks for her escape from shipwreck; in the apse of the church were portraits of emperors of the Theodosian house. In the early sixth century Anicia Juliana, wife and mother of potential emperors, built the church of St Polyeuktos at Constantinople; above its capitals runs an inscription, a poem in praise of her family and her generosity (Brubaker 1997). But it does not follow from these examples that all Christian beneficence was a display of power, a familiar exchange of gift for praise. Even the donors of impressive churches might have assumed that the poor would benefit, because the church would offer shelter and help to those in need.

Did pre-Christian or non-Christian Roman beneficence extend to the very poor? It would be good to think so, but there is little evidence for anything more than individual response to immediate need and official response to crisis (Garnsey and Humfress 2001: 110–23). Roman government did not take general responsibility for welfare, so there was no welfare administration. Local officials took action in emergencies that threatened social order, for instance by releasing grain that was stockpiled for taxes or for the army, or by trying to hire physicians in an epidemic. Local benefactors were also expected to help, and some (like Pliny in his home town of Novum Comum) not only helped in time of crisis, but also tried to improve conditions for local families. But there were no administrative structures to care for people who could not be fed, or nursed, at home. The churches filled that gap, with increasing support from the imperial government as Biblical models of the good king made care for the poor part of the expected imperial role.

'YOU WIN, GALILAEAN'?

Julian recognised welfare provision, and the religious organisation that supported it, as one aspect of Christian practice that could usefully be grafted on to the traditional religion (ch. 2). But he died after only eighteen months as emperor, having failed to revive what he saw as traditional religion, and in the next century, Christian authors claimed that his last words were 'you win, Galilaean!' (*vicisti Galilaee*: see ch. 2 for Julian's use of 'Galilaean'). Had Christianity won, if only by default? Julian complained, in a pamphlet addressed to the people of Antioch, that priests had already forgotten the rituals of sacrifice, and that his own Homeric hecatomb, the sacrifice of a hundred cattle, prompted only complaints about food shortage. Perhaps the Antiochenes were unimpressed by (literal) overkill at a time when Julian's army had already depleted food supplies; or perhaps only a few people cared about the restoration of sacrifice. Some philosophers defended sacrifice as an appropriate offering to the gods who manage this world: that is the argument of Iamblichus, *On the Mysteries* and of Sallustius, *The Gods and the World*. Other philosophers, since the sixth century BCE, had argued that gods do not want blood sacrifice or extravagant offerings, and that people who want to honour the gods may do so modestly, with incense or cakes or flowers, or better still with hymns and prayers and wordless meditation.

How much 'paganism' survived, and for how long (Chuvin 1990)? Julian had to pretend he was Christian until he achieved imperial power: did Christians persecute pagans when they had the chance? In practice, action depended, as with Christian martyrdom (ch. 3), on who was involved, when and where (Salzman 1987; Digeser 2000: 167–71). Eusebius (*VC* 2.44) describes a law, soon after Constantine's defeat of Licinius in 324, forbidding governors to sacrifice, and characteristically interprets it (2.45) as a ban on any sacrifice. In 341 Constantine's son Constantius II banned sacrifice (*C. Th.* 16.10.2), saying that it was contrary to a law of Constantine. But in 342 he wrote to the urban prefect (*C. Th.* 16.10.3) that 'although superstition [i.e. unacceptable cult, ch. 2] must be abolished, we nevertheless wish temple buildings situated outside the walls to remain intact. For plays, circuses and contests originate from several of them, and it would be inappropriate to demolish the source of traditional enjoyments of the Roman people.' In 357 Constantius visited Rome, and his benign attitude to traditional Roman religion was used almost thirty years later as an example to the pious emperor Gratian, who in 382 withdrew funding from traditional cults and priesthoods. Symmachus, prefect of the city, argued in a state paper (*relatio*) for the restoration of funding, and instanced Constantius:

He took nothing from the privileges of the holy virgins [the Vestals]. He filled the priesthoods with nobles. He did not refuse funding for Roman ceremonies. The joyful Senate led the way through the streets of the eternal city, and his face was calm as he saw the shrines; he read the names of the gods inscribed on their pediments; he asked about the origins of the temples and expressed his admiration of their founders. He observed other religious duties himself, but he preserved these for the empire. (Symmachus, *Relationes* 3.7)

This 'heritage' argument was useful in other contexts. Also in 382, the governor of Osrhoene, near the Persian border, was authorised to keep open a temple that was used for assemblies and that contained 'images . . . which may be judged by their artistic value more than by their divinity' (*C. Th.* 16.10.8).

Ten years later, Theodosius I (see above) comprehensively banned the visible practice, public or private, of traditional religion: but there is a question how effectively this law was, or could be, enforced. In 399, at Ravenna, his sons reaffirmed the ban on sacrifice, but also wanted 'the adornments of public buildings' to be preserved, and temples in the countryside to be demolished 'without disturbance or upheaval' (*CT* 16.10.15–16). This sounds like a contradiction in terms, but they probably wanted to avoid the kind of disruption caused by the praetorian prefect Cynegius, assisted by militant monks, in his tour of the east in 386 (Libanius, *Pro Templis* 30.8; Fowden 1978). But also in 399, in Carthage, Gaudentius and Jovius, senior officials (*comites*) of the emperor Honorius, demolished temples and broke up statues; other images of the gods were hurriedly hidden (Aug. *CD* 18.54; Lancel 2002: 221–2). The 'heritage' debate raises the wider question of what counts as secular tradition and what is unacceptable religious practice (Markus 1990; C. Harrison 2000: 132–40). Augustine had to deal with an episode at Calama, in 408, when a traditional procession turned into provocation against Christians and then into outright attack (Atkins and Dodaro 2001: 1–22).

Increasing pressure on the traditional religion was not a reversal of the earlier persecution of Christians: pagans were not tried and executed for their insistence on sacrificing or for their refusal to worship the Christian god. The laws forbidding traditional religious practice are vague about 'divine and human penalties', and even the heavy fines prescribed for officials are not known to have been imposed in the fourth and fifth centuries. Augustine, preaching in North Africa, described a man who says 'by Mercury!', notices a soldier in plain clothes, and hastily adds 'It wasn't me, I wasn't there, I didn't sacrifice' (*Ser. Mainz* 9.8). That sounds alarming; but a little later, also in North Africa, Romans of higher social status were not afraid to declare their traditional beliefs. When disaffected Goths sacked Rome, in 410, many Romans blamed Christian neglect of traditional worship. Some of them took refuge in Carthage, and the imperial commissioner Marcellinus asked Augustine for an impressive response to anti-Christian complaints and 'open letters' setting out the familiar arguments against Christian doctrine. There is no suggestion that it was dangerous to make such complaints.

In the last years of Augustine's life, Macrobius expounded the glories of Roman religious tradition, with special reference to Virgil and with a dramatic setting in late fourth-century Rome. He did not mention Christianity; nor did Symmachus and Claudian in the late fourth century or Martianus Capella in the fifth. They may have been opposed to Christianity; or perhaps, like Augustine's friend Alypius before they were both baptised (*Conf.* 9.4.7), they thought it inappropriate for writing in the classical tradition to include Christian references. In Athens and Alexandria and the cities of the eastern Mediterranean, philosophers continued to lecture on Platonism, to interpret the gods of Hellenic culture as authentic symbols of the divine, and to impress their students with their spiritual power (Chuvin 1990: 101–8). Their lecture-audiences included Christians and non-Christians. This tradition continued into the fifth and sixth centuries, and the story that Justinian closed the Academy of Plato is as much a misrepresentation as the story that Julian forbade Christians to teach or to be taught. Once again, it was a question of access to public funding (Blumenthal 1996: 37–47).

Symmachus, arguing for the restoration of funding to traditional cults, said that there must be more than one route to the highest mystery (*Rel.* 3.10). Pagans and Christians did not have to be sharply opposed.

Philosophers taught, following Plato, that there is one God who is perfectly good; human beings are linked with God through their God-given reason, through lesser divine beings (*daimones*) who act as intermediaries, and through human beings who have so close a connection with God that they are godlike. Ammianus, the admirer of Julian, offered (21.14.5) Apollonius of Tyana, Plotinus and Hermes Trismegistus (ch. 5) as examples of these godlike humans. Such 'soft monotheist' (ch. 1) teachings could also accept Jesus Christ as someone, but not the only one, very close to God; and some Christians were prepared to accept that philosophy at its best came close to Christian understanding of humans in relation to God. The first verse of the Bible, 'In the beginning God created heaven and earth', presented philosophical problems about the relationship of God to the world. But Plato described in the *Timaeus* (of all his dialogues, the one most studied by Christians) how the world was made by the *dēmiourgos*, the creator god. Stoics developed arguments that the organising principle of the world is the *logos* of God, that is, God's thought; Christians argued that Christ is that *logos*. Plato recognised in the *Symposium* the need for mediation between divine and human, and explained how *daimones*, lesser divine beings, fulfilled this role. When Augustine wrote *City of God*, in the early fifth century, he argued that *daimōn*, in current usage, always meant 'demon' (ch. 1). The difference between *daimones* and angels, he said, is that *daimones* want worship for themselves, whereas angels want worship for God; Platonists, who come so close to the truth, should recognise Christ as the true mediator. Christian debates on creation and incarnation continued to use the vocabulary and the thought-patterns of philosophical debates on the relationship between the One and the world, the soul and the body (Stead 1994).

At a different intellectual level, local saints and martyrs could fill the role of local deities, and the 'patron saint' continued the social patterns of the Roman empire (ch. 3). Christian preaching shows that it was only too easy, in Antioch and Constantinople in the time of John Chrysostom, or in Carthage and Hippo Regius in the time of Augustine, for Christians to accommodate their Christianity to Roman society. Some of Augustine's congregation showed a devotion to saints and martyrs that looked to non-Christians very much like worship of lesser gods; some of John Chrysostom's congregation used amulets, rather than prayer, against illness. Paulinus of Nola adapted the tradition of animal sacrifice so that farmers could continue to make an offering, but in honour of St Felix and for distribution to the poor (Trout 1999: 179). Christians got drunk at the feast-days of martyrs just as they did on traditional festivals. Christian pilgrimage to local holy places was an occasion for trouble just as festivals were, and Augustine was not the only bishop who had doubts about the value of long-distance pilgrimage, of seeing with one's own eyes the Holy Land or the living saint (Frank 2000). Christians took food and wine to the tombs of their dead: Ambrose banned this practice because it looked like offerings to the spirits of the dead (Aug. *Conf.* 6.2.2). Christians were missing from church because there was a festival, or games, or something to see at the theatre. The men did not respond well when told to be faithful to their wives: 'My slave-woman is my concubine: would you rather I seduced another man's wife, or went off to the brothel? Can't I do what I like in my own house?' (Aug. *Ser.* 224.3). Many pagans and nominal Christians declined to make the commitment to baptism, or even to become catechumens under instruction: 'tomorrow, tomorrow', they croaked (*cras ero Christianus, cras, cras*: Aug. *Ser. Mainz* 61.27).

How much had changed? There are some simple answers to that question. Christians were not at risk of persecution, and some of them were making efforts to provide religious and moral instruction for all who wanted it, and food, clothing and care for all who needed it. As always, not enough of them were doing this; John Chrysostom told his congregation that with quite modest levels of charitable giving, they could eliminate poverty in Antioch. But at least they tried, and no one has yet shown that non-Christian Roman society made any such effort. Christians have been accused of persecuting in their turn, and of spreading doctrinal intolerance and religious polemic through the pluralist Roman world (Athanassiadi 2002). There were indeed some disgraceful cases of lynching and destruction of property (Fowden 1978), including the murder of the woman philosopher Hypatia, which was so appalling that one group of Christians blamed it on another (Dzielska 1995). The people who did these things were not always punished as they should have been. But mob violence did not result in 'pagans to the lion' (ch. 3). By 423 (*CT* 16.8.26) a Christian emperor could refer to 'the decrees by which We have repressed the spirit and the audacity of the abominable pagans, Jews and indeed heretics' (ch. 1), but legal rhetoric is much more in evidence than formal punishment. Christians were more likely to use violence against Christians than against pagans, in disputes about the expression of faith and about rival claims to religious office. It has been said that more Christians were persecuted for their beliefs after the 'edict of Milan' than before it (Fredriksen and Reinhartz 2002: 27).

Did Christianity transform Roman society, or did Roman society transform Christianity? Either case can be argued, and in either case the transformation could be for the better or for the worse. A society in which the social elite managed politics and law and religion, monopolised education and disregarded the underclass, was brought to recognise the love of God for all human beings, to acknowledge spiritual as well as social authority, and to see the need for moral instruction and welfare provision. Or a tolerant, inclusive society, in which religious practice expressed the commitment of the elite to the community, was persuaded into religious intolerance and the devaluation of family, city and culture. A tiny religious splinter group endured persecution and internal disruption to spread the love of God and love of neighbour throughout the Roman world. Or a simple faith that taught love of God and love of neighbour took on the worst characteristics of empire, with political bishops and violent internal disputes and diversion of funds into display.

A different image may be more helpful than these sharp oppositions. In 354, in the city of Rome, a calendar in fine calligraphy was produced for a distinguished Roman (Salzman 1990). It lists Roman festivals honouring the gods and the emperor; the date of Easter (according to the Roman calculation) from 312 CE for the next fifty years; the bishops of Rome and their places of burial; the calendar of Roman martyrs; and a Christian chronicle. In the *Chronicle* of Eusebius, Biblical history ran, literally, parallel with Roman history and other Mediterranean historical sequences, arranged in parallel columns: the purpose was to show the antiquity of Christian tradition and to integrate the Bible with secular history. Such integration of Christianity and Roman society seemed quite possible in the mid-fourth century.

We are much better informed about the Christian perspective, for the Galilaean did win, the Christian texts were copied, and Christian concerns came to dominate the historical record. But why accept the opposition of Christian and Roman? Christians were Romans in language and culture, and the 'Fathers of the Church' are the Christian writers who were educated in the rhetoric and the philosophy of the Roman empire. When Roman government ended in the west, Roman culture continued because Christian bishops preached in Latin and wrote elegant Latin letters, and because 'barbarian' rulers who were also Christians adopted some elements of Roman culture. In the east, the Byzantine empire continued Roman government and culture for many more centuries. Late antiquity looks different from the classical world: towns focus on churches not temples, their civic buildings are in disrepair or looted for building materials, their countryside is populated with monasteries and shrines of saints. Education came to be based on the Bible, not the classical literary canon. In the sixth century, bishop Agapetus of Rome tried to establish professors of

Biblical studies at Rome, and Cassiodorus, following Augustine's *Christian Teaching*, advocated the study of those classical works that were useful for the understanding of scripture. But Christianity and classical culture are ways that never entirely parted (ch. 1), for classical style and classical learning were constantly rediscovered. Augustine was right: religious believers cannot separate themselves from the society of which they are part. Their beliefs may lead them to challenge some of the aspirations and the practices of that society, but they do not live in a separate city, speaking a distinct language and following distinct customs.

Bibliographical essay

The best approach to the interaction of Christianity and Roman society is to read some of the astonishing range of literature that survives from the early centuries CE. There are several series of lively translations with excellent introductions and commentaries, of which the following are examples.

The Early Church Fathers (Routledge) offers a long introduction to selected texts in translation, and includes Ambrose (B. Ramsey 1997), John Chrysostom (W. Mayer and P. Allen 1999), and Jerome (S. Rebenich 2002).

The Fathers of the Church (Catholic University of America): the older translations vary in quality, but recent volumes have good introductions and annotation.

Translated Texts for Historians (Liverpool University Press): scholarly annotated translations of texts from c. 300 to c. 900.

Penguin Classics include *Early Christian Lives* (tr. C. White, 1998); Oxford World's Classics include *Augustine, Confessions* (tr. H. Chadwick, 1992) and *Christian Teaching* (tr. R. Green, 1995). *Augustine, City of God* is available in paperback from Penguin (tr. H. Bettenson, 1972) and from Cambridge University Press (tr. R. Dyson, 1998).

Augustine for the 21st Century (series editor John E. Rotelle, OSA) aims to provide modern translations, with introductions, of all the works of Augustine; the volumes of sermons (tr. E. Hill, OP) are especially lively.

The Loeb Classical Library (Harvard) offers texts with facing translation, introduction, and brief annotation, and includes works by Philo, Clement of Alexandria, Tertullian, Julian, and letters of Basil, Jerome and Augustine. In the older volumes, the style of the translation can be difficult for present-day students; this also applies to some translations that are available on the Internet because they were out of copyright.

More and more texts and translations are available on the Internet. There are some excellent academic sites; Internet users should, as always, check the credentials of sites and web pages.

Several recent sourcebooks, all with extensive bibliographies, help to locate Christianity within the religious diversity of the Roman empire. Beard–North–Price, *Religions of Rome* (1998) has transformed the study of Roman religion: both the history (vol. 1) and the sourcebook (vol. 2) include material on Jews and Christians. Price's volume in Key Themes in Ancient History, *Religions of the*

Ancient Greeks (1999), includes Jewish and Christian responses to Greek religion. Beard–North–Price extends into late antiquity, but most of the material comes from the late Roman republic and early empire (first century BCE to second century CE). Three sourcebooks specifically on late antiquity, all published in 2000, are helpfully compared in a review by Trout (*BMCR* 01.07.2000). Lee, *Pagans and Christians in Late Antiquity* ranges from the first to the sixth centuries, and is designed for ancient historians rather than for students of church history and theology; Jews, Zoroastrians and Manicheans have a separate section. Maas, *Readings in Late Antiquity* extends more widely over social, political and religious history, including the seventh-century beginnings of Islam. Valantasis, *Religions of Late Antiquity in Practice* is a thematic collection, including Judaism, Christianity, Mithraism, the worship of Isis, and Neoplatonic philosophy.

Edited collections of papers, and some monographs, discuss relationships and debates among these religious options. Christianity in relation to Roman-period Judaism, and Judaism in relation to Roman culture, are discussed by Fredriksen (2000) and Schwartz (2001), and further explored in single-author collections of papers by Rajak (2001) and J. Lieu (2002). Hopkins (1999) shows a special sympathy for the more eccentric variants of Roman, Christian and Jewish religion in the first and second centuries, and combines conventional academic writing with 'classics for the media' as a way of making students think about stories and narratives. Mitchell (1993) integrates archaeology, epigraphy and textual studies in his analysis of Anatolia and its religions, and (as in his paper in Athanassiadi and Frede 1999) shows how difficult it is to make sharp distinctions among pagans, Jews and Christians. Lane Fox (1986) offers a vivid and sympathetic account of traditional civic cult; Liebeschuetz (2000) points to a 'common mood' of monotheism in the early centuries CE and to a shared emphasis on revealed texts, ethics, and life after death. The essays in Athanassiadi and Frede (1999) offer examples of 'soft monotheism', especially in philosophy. The long tradition of work on late Platonism in relation to Christian theology is well represented by the collected papers of Armstrong (1990), Dillon (1991), Markus (1983, 1994), and O'Daly (2001), and, specifically on Augustine, Rist (1994). Many of these discussions also present pagan reservations about Christianity. Wilken (rev. edn 2003) examines the pagan perspective; Digeser (2000) compares the Christian philosopher Lactantius and his anti-Christian contemporary Porphyry. Edwards, Goodman and Price (1999) asked their contributors to consider 'the defence of a religion against actual or perceived opponents': most of the relevant texts are Christian, but the volume includes papers on Jewish and pagan material.

Shared culture is also a theme of recent work. Christian art and architecture used the vocabulary of Graeco-Roman visual culture, and could be differently interpreted by different viewers: White (1990) and Elsner (1998, 2003) explain this approach, Mathews (1999) offers a more controversial interpretation of imagery. Most library systems locate Roman-period Christian texts in Theology not in Classics, but recent work recognises that Christian authors shared the classical education in literature and philosophy. Kaster (1988), Athanassiadi (1992), Brown (1992) and Young (1997) are all illuminating on the purpose and effects of late antique education: Kaster is especially concerned with the use of language, Athanassiadi with philosophy, Brown with rhetoric and Young with exegesis of texts. Rousseau (1994), on Basil, and Brown (2000), on Augustine, discuss two brilliant students and teachers who used rhetoric and exegesis to promote Christianity. Brown 2000 is a revised edition of his pioneering study, published in 1967, which presented Augustine as a man of late antique culture.

Rousseau (2001) explores Christian experience in the Roman world to the time of Gregory the Great (early sixth century); each chapter ends with a small-scale bibliographical essay and helpfully singles out one work as 'where to begin'. His approach, as a historian familiar with and sympathetic to Christian tradition, connects with an earlier tradition of scholarship that is still widely used. Generations of theology students did their early church history from 'Chadwick and Stevenson-Frend'. Chadwick 1967 (and numerous reprints) is a concise and elegant survey of doctrine and practice from the earliest churches to the time of Augustine (early fifth century); he has recently contributed the first and second volumes (2001, 2003) to the ongoing *Oxford History of Christianity*. Frend, a pioneer in the use of archaeological evidence, has also written classic syntheses (1965, rev. edn 1982, and 1984). He restructured and reedited Stevenson's two source-collections (1987, 1989), which provide brief commentary on each (translated) source-extract, time-charts, and notes on sources. Hall (1991) provides a companion to 'Stevenson–Frend'.

Changing perspectives on late antique Roman society include revaluation of the impact of Constantine. Debate has been reopened by Drake 2000, whose Constantine wants consensus politics and religious toleration, but has to engage with intolerant bishops. T. Barnes (1981 and 1982) aims to establish the basic framework of chronology and prosopography that makes interpretation possible. Cameron and Hall (1999) translate, with commentary, the key text *Eusebius: Life of Constantine*. Recent work on the fourth-century church emphasises the social role of bishops as community leaders and patrons. Two outstanding studies of individual bishops, both published in 1994, offer contrasting interpretations: McLynn on Ambrose of Milan presents religion as the pursuit of political aims, Rousseau on Basil of Caesarea presents politics as one concern, but not the central concern, of a religious leader. Hunt (1998), and Garnsey and Humfress (2001), are excellent introductions to the churches in this period. Markus (1990) considers the central questions of 'Christianisation', asking what can be identified as Christian and what counts as secular; C. Harrison (2000) sets Augustine's theology in the context of a society that was not yet Christian. MacMullen (1997) argues for continuity of religious practice; Brown (2002) challenges the distinction between traditional benefaction and Christian charity. In the 1980s it was the world-renouncing Christian ascetics who attracted attention, especially in relation to sexuality, transformations of gender-roles, and attitudes to food and to the body. Wide-ranging surveys include Brown (1988) on sexual renunciation, T. Shaw (1998) on food, Cloke (1995) and Kuefler (2001) on gender-roles, and the sources in Wimbush (1990) and papers in Wimbush (1995). Attention has since moved back to Christians who were part of Roman society: Hunter (1993, 1999) discusses the beliefs of Christians who did not reject Roman society, and Salzman (2002) discusses the accommodation of Christian and traditional concerns in the senatorial aristocracy.

For those not familiar with Roman history or Christian theology, the *Oxford Classical Dictionary* (edn 3, 1996) and *Oxford Dictionary of the Christian Church* (edn 3, 1997) combine to provide an introduction to most relevant people and subjects, and the *Oxford Bible Commentary* (2000) is a lucid single-volume introduction to Christian sacred texts. There are useful survey chapters in the *Cambridge Ancient History* vols. x to xiv and in the *Cambridge History of Judaism* vol. iii. Bowersock, Brown and Grabar (1999) does not claim to be a full encyclopaedia, but includes both encyclopaedia-style entries and introductory essays on a range of subjects. All these works offer bibliographies and directions to the most important texts.

References

Alexander, L. (2002) 'Foolishness to the Greeks: Jews and Christians in the public life of the empire', in Clark and Rajak 2002, 229–49

Archer, L., Fischler, S. and Wyke, M. (1994) *Women in Ancient Societies: an Illusion of the Night* (London)

Arjava, A. (1996) *Women and Law in Late Antiquity* (Oxford)

Armstrong, A. H. (1990) *Hellenic and Christian Studies* (Aldershot)

Ascough, R. (1997) 'Translocal relationships among voluntary organisations and early Christianity', *Journal of Early Christian Studies* 5: 223–41

Athanassiadi, P. (1992) *Julian: an Intellectual Biography* (London)
  (1999) *Damascius: the Philosophical History, a Newly Edited Text with Translation and Notes* (Athens)
  (2002) 'The creation of orthodoxy in Neoplatonism', in Clark and Rajak 2002, 271–91

Athanassiadi, P. and Frede, M., eds. (1999) *Pagan Monotheism in Late Antiquity* (Oxford)

Atkins, E. M. and Dodaro, R. (2001) *Augustine's Political Writings* (Cambridge)

Barnes, J. (2002) 'Ancient Philosophers', in Clark and Rajak 2002, 293–306

Barnes, T. D. (1968) 'Legislation against the Christians', *Journal of Roman Studies* 58: 32–50
  (1981) *Constantine and Eusebius* (Cambridge, MA)
  (1982) *The New Empire of Diocletian and Constantine* (Cambridge, MA)
  (rev. edn 1985) *Tertullian: a Historical and Literary Study* (Oxford)
  (2001) 'Monotheists all?' Review-discussion of Edwards–Goodman–Price 1999 and Athanassiadi and Frede 1999, *Phoenix* 55: 142–62

Barton, S. and Horsley, G. (1981) 'A Hellenistic cult group and the New Testament churches', *Jahrbuch für Antike und Christentum* 24: 7–41

Barton, S. and Muddiman, J., eds. (2000) *The Oxford Bible Commentary* (Oxford)

Bauer, W. (English translation, 1972) *Orthodoxy and Heresy in Earliest Christianity* (London)

Beard, M., North, J. and Price, S. (1998) *Religions of Rome*. Vol. 1: *A History*; Vol. 2: *A Sourcebook* (Cambridge)

Becker, A. and Reed, A. Y., eds. (2003) *The Ways that Never Parted: Jews and Christians in Late Antiquity and the Early Middle Ages* (Tubingen)

BeDuhn, J. (2000) *The Manichean Body in Discipline and Ritual* (Baltimore, MD)

Behr, J. (2000) *Asceticism and Anthropology in Irenaeus and Clement* (Oxford)

Benko, S. (1984) *Pagan Rome and the Early Christians* (Bloomington)

Binns, J. (1994) *Ascetics and Ambassadors of Christ: the Monasteries of Palestine, 314–631* (Oxford)

Blumenthal, H. J. (1996) *Aristotle and Neoplatonism in Late Antiquity* (London)

Bowen, A. and Garnsey, P. (2003) *Lactantius: Divine Institutes* (Liverpool)

Bowersock, G. (1990) *Hellenism in Late Antiquity* (Cambridge, MA)

    (1994) *Fiction as History: Nero to Julian* (Berkeley)

    (1995) *Martyrdom and Rome* (Cambridge)

Bowersock, G., Brown, P., Grabar, A., eds. (1999) *Late Antiquity: a Guide to the Postclassical World* (Cambridge, MA)

Bowman, A., Garnsey, P. and Rathbone, D., eds. (2000) *Cambridge Ancient History* vol. XI: *The Imperial Peace AD 70–192*, 2nd edn (Cambridge)

Boyarin, D. (1999) *Dying for God: Martyrdom and the Making of Christianity and Judaism* (Stanford)

Boyarin, D. and Castelli, E. (2001) 'Introduction: Foucault's *The History of Sexuality*: the fourth volume', *Journal of the History of Sexuality* 10, 357–74

Boys-Stones, G. (2001) *Post-Hellenistic Philosophy: a Study of its Development from the Stoics to Origen* (Oxford)

Bradbury, S. (1996) *Severus of Minorca* (Oxford)

Bradshaw, P. (ed. 2, 2002) *The Search for the Origins of Christian Worship: Sources and Methods for the Study of Early Liturgy* (New York)

Brakke, D. (1995a) *Athanasius and the Politics of Asceticism* (Oxford)

    (1995b) 'The problematization of nocturnal emissions in early Christian Syria, Egypt and Gaul', *Journal of Early Christian Studies* 3.4, 419–60

Brooten, B. (1982) *Women Leaders in the Ancient Synagogue* (Chico)

Brown, P. R. L. (1971) 'The rise and function of the Holy Man in late antiquity', *Journal of Roman Studies* 61: 80–101

    (1981) *The Cult of the Saints: its Rise and Function in Latin Christianity* (Chicago)

    (1988) *The Body and Society: Men, Women and Sexual Renunciation in Early Christianity* (London)

    (1992) *Power and Persuasion in Late Antiquity: towards a Christian Empire* (Madison)

    (rev. edn 2000) *Augustine of Hippo* (London)

    (2002) *Poverty and Leadership in the Later Roman Empire* (Hanover and London)

Brubaker, L. (1997) 'Memories of Helena: patterns in imperial female matronage in the fourth and fifth centuries', in James 1997, 52–75

Burns, T. and Eadie, J., eds. (2001) *Urban Centers and Rural Contexts in Late Antiquity* (Michigan)

Burrus, V. (1995) 'Reading Agnes: the rhetoric of gender in Ambrose and Prudentius', *Journal of Early Christian Studies* 3: 25–46

Burton, P. (2000) *The Old Latin Gospels: a Study of their Texts and Language* (Oxford)

Bynum, C. W. (1995) *The Resurrection of the Body in Western Christianity, 200–1336* (New York)

Cameron, A. (1986) 'Redrawing the map: early Christian territory after Foucault', *Journal of Roman Studies* 76: 266–71

(1991) *Christianity and the Rhetoric of Empire: the Development of Christian Discourse* (Berkeley, CA)

(1994) 'Early Christianity and the discourse of female desire', in Archer–Fischler–Wyke 1994, 152–68

(1996) 'Neither male nor female' (1st publ. 1980), with additional notes, in McAuslan and Walcot 1996, 26–35

Cameron, A. and Hall, S. (1999) *Eusebius: Life of Constantine* (Oxford)

Cameron, A. and Garnsey, P., eds. (1998) *The Cambridge Ancient History* vol. XIII: *The Late Empire, AD 337–425* (Cambridge)

Cameron, A., Ward-Perkins, B. and Whitby, M., eds. (2001) *The Cambridge Ancient History* vol. XIV: *Late Antiquity: Empire and Successors, AD 425–600* (Cambridge)

Campbell, J. (2nd edn, 2002) *Deciphering the Dead Sea Scrolls* (Oxford)

Castelli, E. (1998) 'Gender, theory, and *The Rise of Christianity*: a response to Rodney Stark', *Journal of Early Christian Studies* 6.2: 227–58

Chadwick, H. (1965) *Origen: Against Celsus* (Oxford)

(1967 and reprints) *The Early Church* (Harmondsworth)

(1976) *Priscillian of Avila: the Occult and the Charismatic in the Early Church* (Oxford)

(2001) *The Church in Ancient Society: from Galilee to Gregory the Great* (Oxford)

(2003) *East and West: the Making of a Rift in the Church – from Apostolic Times until the Council of Florence* (Oxford)

Chuvin, P. (1990) *A Chronicle of the Last Pagans* (Cambridge, MA)

Clark, E. A. (1986) *Ascetic Piety and Women's Faith* (New York)

(1999) *Reading Renunciation: Asceticism and Scripture in Early Christianity* (Princeton)

Clark, G. (1993) *Women in Late Antiquity: Pagan and Christian Lifestyles* (Oxford)

(1994) 'The Fathers and the Children', in Wood 1994, 1–28

(1996) 'The bright frontier of friendship: Augustine and the Christian body as frontier', in Mathisen and Sivan 1996, 217–29

(1998a) 'Bodies and blood: martyrdom, virginity and resurrection in late antiquity', in Montserrat 1998, 99–115

(1998b) 'The old Adam: patristics and the (un)making of masculinity', in Foxhall and Salmon 1998, 170–82

(1999a) 'Victricius of Rouen: *Praising the Saints*', *Journal of Early Christian Studies* 7.3: 365–99

(1999b) 'Translate into Greek: Porphyry of Tyre and the new barbarians', in Miles 1999, 112–32

(2000a) *Porphyry: On Abstinence from Eating Animals* (London)

(2000b) 'Philosophic *Lives* and the philosophic life', in Hägg and Rousseau 2000, 29–51

(2001a) 'Translating relics: Victricius of Rouen and fourth-century debate', *Early Medieval Europe* 10 (2): 161–76

(2001b) 'Pastoral care: town and country in late-antique preaching', in Burns and Eadie 2001, 265–84

(fc a) 'The health of the spiritual athlete', in King fc

(fc b) 'In the foreskin of their flesh: the pure male body in late antiquity' in Hopkins and Wyke fc

Clark, G. and Rajak, T., eds. (2002) *Philosophy and Power in the Graeco-Roman World* (Oxford)

Cloke, G. (1995) *This Female Man of God: Women and Spiritual Power in the Patristic Age, AD 350–450* (London)

Cohen, S. (1993) 'Those who say they are Jews and are not', in Cohen and Frerichs 1993, 1–45

Cohen, S. and Frerichs, E., eds. (1993) *Diasporas in Antiquity* (Atlanta, GA)

Coleman, K. (1990) 'Fatal charades: Roman executions staged as mythological enactments', *Journal of Roman Studies* 80: 44–73

Coleman-Norton, P. R. (1966) *Roman State and Christian Church: a Collection of Legal Documents to AD 535* (London)

Conybeare, C. (2000) *Paulinus Noster: Self and Symbols in the Letters of Paulinus of Nola* (Oxford)

Cooper, K. (1996) *The Virgin and the Bride: Idealized Womanhood in Late Antiquity* (Cambridge, MA)

Copenhaver, B. P. (1992) *Hermetica: the Greek Corpus Hermeticum and the Latin Asclepius in a New English Translation with Notes and Introduction* (Cambridge)

Countryman, L. (1980) *The Rich Christian in the Church of the Early Empire* (New York)

Cramer, P. (1993) *Baptism and Change in the Early Middle Ages, c. 200 – c. 1150* (Cambridge)

Curran, J. (2000) *Pagan City and Christian Capital: Rome in the Fourth Century* (Oxford)

Davidson, I. (2001) *Ambrose: De Officiis* (Oxford)

Davis, R. (1989) *The Book of Pontiffs (Liber Pontificalis): the Ancient Biographies of the First Ninety Roman Bishops to AD 715* (Liverpool)

Delehaye, H., S. J. (1905; English translation 1961) *The Legends of the Saints* (Notre Dame)

Digeser, E. (2000) *The Making of a Christian Empire: Lactantius and Rome* (Ithaca)

Dillon, J. (1991) *The Golden Chain: Studies in the Development of Platonism and Christianity* (Aldershot)

Dionisotti, C. (1982) 'From Ausonius' schooldays? A schoolbook and its relatives', *Journal of Roman Studies* 72: 83–125

Dodds, E. R. (1965) *Pagan and Christian in an Age of Anxiety* (Cambridge)

Dolbeau, F. (1996) *Augustin d'Hippone: vingt-six sermons au peuple d'Afrique* (Paris)

Doran, R. (1992) *The Lives of Symeon Stylites* (Kalamazoo)

Drake, H. A. (2000) *Constantine and the Bishops: the Politics of Intolerance* (Baltimore)

Dzielska, M. (1995) *Hypatia of Alexandria* (Cambridge, MA)

Edwards, M. (1997) *Optatus: Against the Donatists* (Liverpool)
  (2000) *Neoplatonic Saints: the Lives of Plotinus and Proclus by their Students* (Liverpool)
  (2003) *Constantine and Christendom* (Liverpool)
Edwards, M., Goodman, M., Price, S., eds. (1999) *Apologetics in the Roman Empire: Pagans, Jews and Christians* (Oxford)
Edwards, M., and Swain, S., eds. (1997) *Portraits: Biographical Representation in Greek and Latin Literature of the Roman Empire* (Oxford)
Elm, S. (1994) *Virgins of God: the Making of Asceticism in Late Antiquity* (Oxford)
  (1998) 'Introduction', *Journal of Early Christian Studies* 6: 343–51
Elsner, J. (1998) *Imperial Rome and Christian Triumph* (Oxford)
  (2003) 'Archaeologies and agendas: reflections on late ancient Jewish art and early Christian art', *Journal of Roman Studies* 93: 114–28
Esler, P. (1994) *The First Christians in their Social World: Social-Scientific Approaches to New Testament Interpretation* (London)
  ed. (2000) *The Early Christian World* (London)
Evans Grubbs, J. (1995) *Law and Family in Late Antiquity: the Emperor Constantine's Marriage Legislation* (Oxford)
Fiorenza, E. S. (1983) *In Memory of Her: a Feminist Theological Reconstruction of Christian Origins* (London)
Fowden, G. (1978) 'Bishops and temples in the eastern Roman empire AD 320–425', *Journal of Theological Studies* 29: 53–78
  (1982) 'The pagan holy man in late antique society', *Journal of Hellenic Studies* 102: 33–59
  (1986) *The Egyptian Hermes: a Historical Approach to the Late Pagan Mind* (Cambridge)
  (1993) *Empire to Commonwealth: Consequences of Monotheism in Late Antiquity* (Princeton)
  (1998) 'Polytheist religion and philosophy', in Cameron and Garnsey 1998, 538–60
Foxhall, L. and Salmon, J., eds. (1998) *Thinking Men: Masculinity and its Self-Representation in the Classical Tradition* (London)
Frank, G. (2000) *The Memory of the Eyes: Pilgrims to Living Saints in Christian Late Antiquity* (Berkeley)
Frede, M. (1999) 'Origen's treatise *Against Celsus*', in Edwards–Goodman–Price 1999, 131–55
Fredriksen, P. (2000) *From Jesus to Christ* (second edition, New Haven and London)
Fredriksen, P. and Reinhartz, A. eds. (2002) *Jesus, Judaism and Christian Anti-Judaism* (Louisville and London)
Frend, W. (1965, revised 1982) *The Early Church: from the Beginnings to 461* (London)
  (1984) *The Rise of Christianity* (London)
Gamble, H. (1995) *Books and Readers in the Early Church: a History of Early Christian Texts* (New Haven and London)
Garnsey, P. (1970) *Social Status and Legal Privilege in the Roman Empire* (Cambridge)
  (1996) *Ideas of Slavery from Aristotle to Augustine* (Cambridge)
  (1999) *Food and Society in Classical Antiquity* (Cambridge)

Garnsey, P. and Humfress, C. (2001) *The Evolution of the Late Antique World* (Cambridge)

Gleason, M. (1998) 'Visiting and news: gossip and reputation management in the desert', *Journal of Early Christian Studies* 6.3: 501–21

Goldhill, S. (1995) *Foucault's Virginity: Ancient Erotic Fiction and the History of Sexuality* (Cambridge)

Goodman, M. (1994) *Mission and Conversion: Proselytizing in the Religious History of the Roman Empire* (Oxford)

(1999) 'Josephus' treatise *Against Apion*', in Edwards–Goodman–Price 1999, 45–58

Goodman, M. with Cohen, J. and Sorkin, D. (2002) *The Oxford Handbook of Jewish Studies* (Oxford)

Gould, G. (1993) *The Desert Fathers on Monastic Community* (Oxford)

Griffin, M. (2003) '*De beneficiis* and Roman society', *Journal of Roman Studies* 93: 92–113

Griffin, M. and Atkins, E. M. (1991) *Cicero: On Duties* (Cambridge)

Grimm, V. (1996) *From Feasting to Fasting: the Evolution of a Sin* (London)

Hadot, P. (English translation, 1995) *Philosophy as a Way of Life* (Oxford)

Hägg, T. (1992) 'Hierocles the lover of truth and Eusebius the Sophist', *Symbolae Osloenses* 67: 138–50

ed. (1997) 'SO debate: the world of late antiquity revisited', *Symbolae Osloenses* 72: 5–90

Hägg, T. and Rousseau, P., eds. (2000) *Greek Biography and Panegyric in Late Antiquity* (Berkeley, CA)

Hanson, R. (1989) 'The achievement of orthodoxy in the fourth century AD', in R. Williams 1989b, 142–56

Harries, J. D. (1999a) *Law and Empire in Late Antiquity* (Cambridge)

(1999b) 'Constructing the judge: judicial accountability and the culture of criticism in late antiquity', in Miles 1999, 214–33

Harris, W. V. (1989) *Ancient Literacy* (Cambridge, MA)

Harrison, C. (2000) *Augustine: Christian Truth and Fractured Humanity* (Oxford)

Harrison, S. J. (2000) *Apuleius: a Latin Sophist* (Oxford)

Harvey, S. A. (1992) 'Foreword', in Doran 1992, 7–12

Hayward, P. A. and Howard-Johnson, J., eds. (1999) *The Cult of Saints in Late Antiquity and the Early Middle Ages* (Oxford)

Head, T., ed. (2001) *Medieval Hagiography: an Anthology* (London)

Heather, P. and Matthews, J. (1991) *The Goths in the Fourth Century* (Liverpool)

Heffernan, T. J. (1988) *Sacred Biography: Saints and their Biographers in the Middle Ages* (Oxford / New York)

Helgeland, J., Daly, R. J., and Burns, J. P. (1985) *Christians and the Military: the Early Experience* (London)

Hess, H. (2002) *The Early Development of Canon Law and the Council of Serdica* (Oxford)

Holman, S. (2001) *The Hungry are Dying: Beggars and Bishops in Roman Cappadocia* (Oxford)

Hopkins, K. (1991) 'Conquest by book', in Humphrey 1991, 133–58
  (1998) 'Christian number and its implications', *Journal of Early Christian Studies* 6.2: 185–226
  (1999) *A World Full of Gods* (London)
Hopkins, A. and Wyke, M., eds. *Roman Bodies* (British School at Rome, fc)
Horbury, W., Davies, W. and Sturdy, J., eds. (1999) *The Cambridge History of Judaism*, III : *The Early Roman Period* (Cambridge)
Howard-Johnston, J., and Hayward, P. A., eds. (1999) *The Cult of Saints in Late Antiquity and the Early Middle Ages* (Oxford)
Humphrey, J. H., ed. (1991) *Literacy in the Roman World* (*Journal of Roman Archaeology* supplement)
Humphries, M. (1999) *Communities of the Blessed: Social Environment and Religious Change in Northern Italy, 200–400* (Oxford)
Hunt, E. D. (1982) *Holy Land Pilgrimage in the Later Roman Empire* (Oxford)
  (1998) 'The church as a public institution', in Cameron and Garnsey 1998, 238–76
Hunter, D. (1987) 'Resistance to the virginal ideal in late fourth-century Rome: the case of Jovinian', *Theological Studies* 48: 45–64
  (1989) '*On the Sin of Adam and Eve*: a little known defense of marriage and childbearing by Ambrosiaster', *Harvard Theological Review* 82: 283–99
  (1992) 'The paradise of patriarchy: Ambrosiaster on women as not in God's image', *Journal of Theological Studies* 43: 447–69
  (1993) 'Helvidius, Jovinian, and the virginity of Mary in late fourth-century Rome', *Journal of Early Christian Studies* 1.1: 47–71
  (1999) 'Vigilantius of Calagurris and Victricius of Rouen: ascetics, relics and clerics in late Roman Gaul', *Journal of Early Christian Studies* 7.3: 401–30
James, L., ed. (1997) *Women, Men and Eunuchs: Gender in Byzantium* (London)
James, P. (1999) 'Prudentius' *Psychomachia*: the Christian arena and the politics of display', in Miles 1999, 70–94
Janowitz, N. (1998) 'Rabbis and their opponents: the construction of the "Min" in Rabbinic anecdotes', *Journal of Early Christian Studies* 6.3: 449–62
Jones, C. (1993) 'Women, death and the law in the Christian persecutions', in Wood 1993, 23–34
Kaster, R. (1988) *Guardians of Language: the Grammarian and Society in Late Antiquity* (Berkeley, CA)
Kelly, J. (3rd edn, 1972) *Early Christian Creeds* (London)
  (1975) *Jerome: his Life, Writings and Controversies* (London)
  (1995) *Golden Mouth: the Story of John Chrysostom – Ascetic, Preacher, Bishop* (London)
Kennedy, H. (1999) 'Islam', in Bowersock–Brown–Grabar 1999, 219–37
King, H., ed. (fc a) *Health in Antiquity* (London)
King, H. (fc b) 'Women's health and recovery in the Hippocratic corpus', in King fc a
King, K. (2003) *What is Gnosticism?* (Cambridge, MA)

Klingshirn, W. (1994a) *Caesarius of Arles: the Making of a Christian Community in Late Antique Gaul* (Cambridge)

(1994b) *Caesarius of Arles: Life, Testament, Letters* (Liverpool)

Klingshirn, W. and Vessey, M., eds. (1999) *The Limits of Ancient Christianity: Essays on Late Antique Thought and Culture in Honor of R. A. Markus* (Michigan)

Kraemer, R. S. (1988) *Maenads, Martyrs, Matrons, Monastics: a Sourcebook on Women's Religions in the Greco-Roman World* (Philadelphia)

(1992) *Her Share of the Blessings: Women's Religions among Pagans, Jews and Christians in the Greco-Roman World* (Oxford)

Kuefler, M. (2001) *The Manly Eunuch: Masculinity, Gender Ambiguity, and Christian Ideology in Late Antiquity* (Chicago)

Kyle, D. G. (1998) *Spectacles of Death in Ancient Rome* (London)

Lamberton, R. (1986) *Homer the Theologian* (Berkeley, CA)

Lancel, S. (English translation, 2002) *St Augustine* (London)

Lane Fox, R. (1986) *Pagans and Christians* (Harmondsworth)

(1997) 'The *Life of Daniel*', in Edwards and Swain 1997, 175–225

Lawless, G. (1987) *Augustine of Hippo and his Monastic Rule* (Oxford)

Lawlor, H., and Oulton, J. (1927) *Eusebius, Bishop of Caesarea: the Ecclesiastical History* (London)

Layton, B. (1987) *The Gnostic Scriptures* (London)

Lee, D. (2000) *Pagans and Christians in Late Antiquity* (London)

Liebeschuetz, W. (2000), 'Religion', in Bowman, Garnsey and Rathbone 2000, 984–1008

Lieu, J. (2002) *Neither Jew nor Greek? Constructing Early Christianity* (London)

Lieu, J., North, J. and Rajak, T., eds. (1992) *The Jews among Pagans and Christians* (London)

Lieu, S., ed. (2nd edn, 1989) *The Emperor Julian: Panegyric and Polemic* (Liverpool)

Lieu, S. and Montserrat, D. (1996) *From Constantine to Julian: Pagan and Byzantine views* (London)

(1998) *Constantine: History, Historiography and Legend* (London)

Lieu, S. and Gardner, I. (2003) *Manichaean Texts from the Roman Empire* (Cambridge)

Lim, R. (1995) *Public Disputation, Power and Social Order in Late Antiquity* (Berkeley)

Long, A. (2002) *Epictetus: a Stoic and Socratic Guide to Life* (Oxford)

Louth, A. (2002) *St John Damascene: Tradition and Originality in Byzantine Theology* (Oxford)

Maas, M. (2000) *Readings in Late Antiquity* (London)

MacCormack, S. (1981) *Art and Ceremony in Late Antiquity* (Berkeley, CA)

MacMullen, R. (1984) *Christianizing the Roman Empire, AD 100–400* (New Haven)

(1986) 'What difference did Christianity make?', *Historia* 35: 322–43

(1989) 'The preacher's audience (AD 350–400)', *Journal of Theological Studies* 40: 503–11

(1997) *Christianity and Paganism in the Fourth to Eighth Centuries* (New Haven)

Magnou-Nortier, E. (2002) *Le Code Théodosien, livre* xvi, *et sa réception au Moyen Age* (Paris)

Mango, C. (1990) 'Constantine's Mausoleum and the translation of relics', *Byzantinische Zeitschrift* 83: 51–61

Markus, R. A. (1983) *From Augustine to Gregory the Great: History and Christianity in late antiquity* (Aldershot)

(rev. edn, 1988) *Saeculum: History and Society in the Theology of St Augustine* (Cambridge)

(1990) *The End of Ancient Christianity* (Cambridge)

(1994) *Sacred and Secular: Studies on Augustine and Latin Christianity* (Aldershot)

Mathews, T. F. (1993, rev. edn, 1999) *The Clash of Gods: a Reinterpretation of Early Christian Art* (Princeton)

Mathisen, R. and Sivan, H., eds. (1996) *Shifting Frontiers in Late Antiquity* (Aldershot)

McAuslan, I., and Walcot, P., eds. (1996) *Women in Antiquity: Greece & Rome Studies* 3 (Oxford)

McGowan, A. (1999) *Ascetic Eucharists: Food and Drink in Early Christian Ritual Meals* (Oxford)

McLynn, N. (1994) *Ambrose of Milan: Church and Conflict in a Christian Capital* (Berkeley, CA)

Meeks, W. (1983) *The First Urban Christians: the Social World of the Apostle Paul* (New Haven)

Merdinger, J. (1997) *Rome and the African Church in the Time of Augustine* (New Haven)

Miles, R., ed. (1999) *Constructing Identities in Late Antiquity* (London)

Millar, F. (1977) *The Emperor in the Roman World* (London)

Miller, P. C. (1993) 'The blazing body: ascetic desire in Jerome's letter to Eustochium', *Journal of Early Christian Studies* 1.1: 21–45

(1994) *Dreams in Late Antiquity: Studies in the Imagination of a Culture* (Princeton)

Miller, T. (1985) *The Birth of the Hospital in the Byzantine Empire* (Baltimore)

Mitchell, S. (1993) *Anatolia: Land, Men and Gods in Asia Minor*, 2 vols. (Oxford)

(1999) 'The Cult of Theos Hypsistos between pagans, Jews and Christians', in Athanassiadi and Frede 1999, 81–148

Montserrat, D., ed. (1998) *Changing Bodies, Changing Meanings: Studies on the Human Body in Late Antiquity* (London)

Moxnes, H., ed. (1997) *Constructing Early Christian Families: Family as Social Reality and Metaphor* (London)

Musurillo, H. (1972) *The Acts of the Christian Martyrs* (Oxford)

Nicholson, O. (1994) 'The "pagan churches" of Maximinus Daia and Julian the Apostate', *Journal of Ecclesiastical History* 45: 1–10

Nock, A. D. (1926) *Sallustius: Concerning the Gods and the Universe* (Cambridge)

(1972) *Essays on Religion in the Ancient World*, 2 vols., ed. Z. Stewart (Oxford)

Nutton, V. (1986) Essay-review of T. Miller, *Medical History* 30: 218–21.

O'Daly, G. (2001) *Platonism Pagan and Christian: Studies in Plotinus and Augustine* (Aldershot)

O'Donnell, J. (1992) *Augustine: Confessions*, 3 vols. (Oxford)

O'Meara, D. (2003) *Platonopolis: Platonic Political Philosophy in Late Antiquity* (Oxford)

Osborne, C. (1994) *Eros Unveiled: Plato and the God of Love* (Oxford)

Peers, G. (2001) *Subtle Bodies: Representing Angels in Byzantium* (Berkeley, CA)

Penn, M. (2002) 'Performing family: ritual kissing and the construction of Early Christian kinship', *Journal of Early Christian Studies* 10: 151–74

Perkins, J. (1995) *The Suffering Self: Pain and Narrative Representation in the Early Christian Era* (London)

Potter, D. S.(1990) *Prophecy and History in the Crisis of the Empire: a Historian's Commentary on the Thirteenth Sibylline Oracle* (Oxford)

Price, S. (1999) *Religions of the Ancient Greeks* (Cambridge)

Rajak, T. (1997) 'Dying for the law: the martyr's portrait in Jewish-Greek literature', in Edwards and Swain 1997, 39–67

(1999) 'Talking at Trypho', in Edwards–Goodman–Price 1999, 59–80

(2001) *The Jewish Dialogue with Greece and Rome* (Leiden)

(rev.ed. 2003) *Josephus: the Historian and his Society* (London)

Rebenich, S. (2002) *Jerome* (London)

Rist, J. (1994) *Augustine: Ancient Thought Baptized* (Cambridge)

Rives, J. (1995) 'Human sacrifice among Pagans and Christians', *Journal of Roman Studies* 85: 65–85

(1996) 'The piety of a persecutor', *Journal of Early Christian Studies* 4: 1–25

(1999) 'The decree of Decius and the religion of empire', *Journal of Roman Studies* 89: 135–54

Robert, L. (1994) *Le Martyre de Pionios, prêtre de Smyrne*, ed. G. Bowersock and C. P. Jones (Washington, DC)

Roberts, M. (1993) *Poetry and the Cult of Martyrs* (Michigan)

Robinson, C. (1999), 'Prophecy and holy men in early Islam', in Howard-Johnston and Hayward 1999, 241–62

(2003) *Islamic Historiography* (Cambridge)

Robinson, J. M. (1988) *The Nag Hammadi Library in English*, 3rd edn (Leiden)

Rousseau, P. (1985) *Pachomius: the Making of a Community in Fourth-Century Egypt* (Berkeley, CA)

(1994) *Basil of Caesarea* (Berkeley, CA)

(2002) *The Early Christian Centuries* (London)

Rousselle, A. (English translation, 1988) *Porneia: on Desire and the Body in Antiquity* (Oxford)

Rowland, C. (1985) *Christian Origins: an Account of the Setting and Character of the Most Important Messianic Sect of Judaism* (London)

Russell, N. (2004) *Gods through Grace: the Doctrine of Deification in the Greek Patristic Tradition* (Oxford)

Salisbury, J. (1998) *Perpetua's Passion: the Death and Memory of a Young Roman Woman* (London)

Salzman, M. (1987) '*Superstitio* in the *Codex Theodosianus* and the persecution of pagans', *Vigiliae Christianae* 41: 172–88

(1990) *On Roman Time: the Codex-Calendar of 354 and the Rhythms of Urban Life in Late Antiquity* (Berkeley, CA)

(2002) *The Making of a Christian Aristocracy* (Cambridge, MA)

Schwartz, S. (2001) *Imperialism and Jewish Society, 200 BCE to 640 CE* (Princeton)

Shaw, B. (1993) 'The Passion of Perpetua', *Past and Present* 139: 3–45

(2003) 'Judicial nightmares and Christian memory', *Journal of Early Christian Studies* 11: 533–63

Shaw, T. (1998) *The Burden of the Flesh: Fasting and Sexuality in Early Christianity* (Minneapolis)

Smith, J. (1990) *Drudgery Divine: on the Comparison of Early Christianities and the Religions of Late Antiquity* (London)

Smith, M. (1998) 'Coptic literature, 337–425', in Cameron and Garnsey 1998, 720–35

Smith, R. (1995) *Julian's Gods: Religion and Philosophy in the Thought and Action of Julian the Apostate* (London)

Sorabji, R. (1993) *Animal Minds and Human Morals* (London)

(2000) *Emotion and Peace of Mind: from Stoic Agitation to Christian Temptation* (Oxford)

Stark, R. (1996) *The Rise of Christianity: a Sociologist Reconsiders History* (Princeton)

Stead, C. (1994) *Philosophy in Christian Antiquity* (Cambridge)

Stevenson, J., revised Frend, W. H. C. (1987) *A New Eusebius: Documents Illustrating the History of the Church to AD 337* (London)

revised Frend, W. H. C. (1989) *Creeds, Councils and Controversies: Documents Illustrating the History of the Church AD 337 to 461* (London)

Straw, C. (1999), 'Martyrdom and Christian identity: Gregory the Great, Augustine, and tradition', in Klingshirn and Vessey 1999, 250–66

Swain S. (1997) 'Biography and biographic in the literature of the Roman empire', in Edwards and Swain 1997, 1–37

(1999) 'Defending Hellenism: Philostratus, *In Honour of Apollonius*', in Edwards–Goodman–Price 1999, 157–96

Taylor, J. (2003) *Jewish Women Philosophers of First-Century Alexandria: Philo's 'Therapeutae' Reconsidered* (Oxford)

Thacker, A. (1998) 'Memorializing Gregory the Great: the origin and transmission of a papal cult in the seventh and early eighth centuries', *Early Medieval Europe* 7.1, 59–84

Thacker, A., and Sharpe, R. eds. (2002) *Local Saints and Local Churches in the Early Medieval West* (Oxford)

Tilley, M. (1996) *Donatist Martyr Stories* (Liverpool)

Tomlin, R. (1998) 'Christianity and the late Roman army', in Lieu and Montserrat 1998, 21–51

Trout, D. (1999) *Paulinus of Nola: Life, Letters and Poems* (Berkeley, CA)

Turcan, R. (1996) *The Cults of the Roman Empire* (Oxford)

Valantasis, R., ed. (2000) *Religions of Late Antiquity in Practice* (Princeton)

Van Bremen, R. (1996) *The Limits of Participation: Women and Civic Life in the Greek East in the Hellenistic and Roman Periods* (Amsterdam)

Van Dam, R. (2002) *Kingdom of Snow: Roman Rule and Greek Culture in Cappadocia* (Philadelphia)

Vessey, M. (1998) 'The demise of the Christian writer and the remaking of "Late Antiquity": from H.-I. Marrou's Saint Augustine (1938) to Peter Brown's Holy Man (1983)', *Journal of Early Christian Studies* 6.3: 377–411

Veyne, P. (1976) *Le Pain et le Cirque: sociologie historique d'un pluralisme politique* (Paris) (Engl. tr. (abridged) *Bread and Circuses: Historical Sociology and Political Pluralism* (London, 1990))

Ward, K. (2000) *Christianity: a Short Introduction* (Oxford)

White, L. M. (1990) *Building God's House in the Roman World: Architectural Adaptation among Jews, Pagans and Christians* (Baltimore, MD)

Wickham, L. (1997) *Hilary of Poitiers: Conflicts of Conscience and Law in the Fourth-Century Church* (Liverpool)

Wiedemann, T. J. (1992) *Emperors and Gladiators* (London)

Wilken, R. (1999) 'Cyril of Alexandria's *Contra Iulianum*', in Klingshirn and Vessey 1999, 42–62

Wilken, R. (rev. edn 2003) *The Christians as the Romans Saw Them* (New Haven)

Williams, D. H. (1995) *Ambrose of Milan and the End of the Arian-Nicene Conflicts* (Oxford)

Williams, M. (1996) *Rethinking Gnosticism: an Argument for Dismantling a Dubious Category* (Princeton, NJ)

Williams, R. (1989a) 'Does it make sense to speak of pre-Nicene orthodoxy?', in R. Williams 1989b, 1–23

ed. (1989b) *The Making of Orthodoxy: Essays in Honour of Henry Chadwick* (Cambridge)

(1987, 2nd edn, 2001) *Arius* (London)

(2003) *Silence and Honey Cakes: the Wisdom of the Desert Fathers* (Oxford)

Williamson, G. A. (rev. edn 1989) *Eusebius: the History of the Church* (Harmondsworth)

Wimbush, V., ed. (1990) *Ascetic Behavior in Greco-Roman Antiquity: a Sourcebook* (Minneapolis)

Wimbush, V. and Valantasis, R., eds. (1995) *Asceticism* (Oxford)

Wood, D., ed. (1993) *Martyrs and Martyrologies*, Studies in Church History 30 (Oxford)

ed. (1994) *The Church and Childhood*, Studies in Church History 31 (Oxford)

Wyke, M. (1998a) 'Playing Roman soldiers: the martyred body, Derek Jarman's *Sebastiane*, and the representation of male homosexuality', in Wyke 1998b, 243–66

ed. (1998b) *Parchments of Gender: Deciphering the Bodies of Antiquity* (Oxford)

Young, F. (1983) *From Nicaea to Chalcedon: a Guide to the Literature and its Background* (London)

(1997) *Biblical Exegesis and the Formation of Christian Culture* (Cambridge)

Index